OUR ORIGINAL SCENES
FREUD'S THEORY OF SEXUALITY

FIGURES OF THE UNCONSCIOUS 6

Editorial Board

J. CORVELEYN, P. MOYAERT, PH. VAN HAUTE,
W. VER EECKE, R. BERNET

Our original scenes
Freud's theory of sexuality

Tomas Geyskens

Leuven University Press
2005

Published with the support of the Philosophy Faculty of the Radboud University Nijmegen.

© 2005 Leuven University Press / Universitaire Pers Leuven / Presses Universitaires de Louvain
Blijde Inkomststraat 5, B-3000 Leuven (Belgium)

All rights reserved. Except in those cases expressly determined by law, no part of this publication may be multiplied, saved in an automated datafile or made public in any way whatsoever without the express prior written consent of the publishers.

ISBN 90 5867 471 1
D/ 2005 / 1869 / 29
NUR: 777

Design cover: Lejon Tits
Illustration cover: Goya, Las Gigantillas (© Museo Nacional del Prado. Madrid)

CONTENTS

Introduction—Psychoanalysis as clinical anthropology	7
1. An instinct perverted by beauty—*Three Essays* as a sexual aesthetics	11
2. What is sexual about infantile "sexuality"?	21
3. The constitution of sexual phantasy	29
4. The destruction of sexual phantasy	45
5. Love and need in *Instincts and their vicissitudes*	55
6. The capacity to suffer	63
7. Oedipus: Abandonment and exile	77
8. The Minoan-Mycenaean civilisation	87
9. Freud beyond psychoanalysis?	103

Ich überlasse mich meinen Phantasien, spiele Schach, lese englische Romane;
alles Ernsthafte bleibt verbannt. (Freud)

C'est dans le sein de la mère que se fabriquent les organes qui doivent nous rendre susceptible de telle ou telle fantaisie; les premiers objets présentés, les premiers discours entendus achèvent de déterminer le ressort: l'éducation a beau faire, elle ne change plus rien. (D.A.F de Sade)

I thank Andreas De Block, Paul Moyaert, and Philippe Van Haute for their support and advice.

INTRODUCTION—PSYCHOANALYSIS AS CLINICAL ANTHROPOLOGY

Infantile sexuality is a *construction* based on the analysis of pathologies of adults. The pathologies of his adult patients forced Freud to develop a theory in which these pathologies are traced back to an *infantile factor*. About this infantile factor, Freud says in *A Child is Being Beaten* (1919) that "it has never had a real existence. It is never remembered, it has never succeeded in becoming conscious. It is a construction of analysis, but it is no less a necessity on that account." (Freud 1919, 185) Freud's ideas on infantile sexuality can only be understood as constructions that are necessary to understand the psychopathological formations of adults. These constructions of infantile sexuality, therefore, must not be considered to be speculations about infant behaviour as such, because in infancy sexuality is obviously a rather marginal problem,[1] and because, consequently, only their *nachträglich* effects reveal the significance of our infantile sexual experiences.[2] In the psychoanalytic cure, these infantile experiences are never remembered as such. The idea that what is repressed in adults can be observed in infants does not take into account this notion of *Nachträglichkeit*, while Freud's theory cannot be understood without it. (Green 2000, 149)

Freud's claim that infantile sexuality is the *determining* cause of psychopathology can only be understood within the context of evolutionary biology. This does not imply that Freud is a *biologist of the mind* whose psychology is just a biology transposed onto psychology.[3] Freud's 'biologism' does imply, however, that the problem of anthropological difference (i.e. the difference between humans and the other animals) must ultimately be answered by biology. According to Freud, "the present development of human beings requires, as it seems to me, no different explanation from that of animals." (Freud 1920, 42) In this view, what is specifically human cannot be considered as something super-natural. It is exactly in this naturalistic perspective that psychopathology plays a crucial role. Since perversion is a specifically human

---

[1] "This *postulated* constitution, containing the germs of all the perversions, will only be demonstrable in children, even though *in them it is only with modest degrees of intensity* that any of the instincts can emerge." (Freud 1905, 172, my emphasis)

[2] Laplanche and Pontalis define *Nachträglichkeit* as follows: "Experiences, impressions and memory-traces may be revised at a later date to fit in with fresh experiences or with the attainment of a new stage of development. They may in that event be endowed *not only with a new meaning but also with psychical effectiveness.*" (Laplanche & Pontalis 1988, 111, my emphasis)

[3] This is the claim of Sulloway in his *Freud: Biologist of the Mind* (1979).

phenomenon, there has to be a biological condition for it that is specific for the human animal. According to Freud, the crucial difference between humans and the other animals is the peculiar sexual development of human beings; the two-phased onset of human sexuality.[4]

This two-phased onset of sexuality in human beings (in infancy and puberty) must therefore be the ultimate biological condition for the possibility of psychopathology. In puberty, sexual maturation starts, but it starts for the second time. In infancy, there has already been a first efflorescence of sexuality, i.e. of oral, anal and genital pleasures and of sexual curiosity and phantasy. These infantile phantasies and impulses are re-cathected at puberty. Therefore, the genital urge towards the other sex, which is specific to puberty, is affected by the memory traces of infantile phantasies and impulses that were not directed at genital intercourse or even at the other sex. According to Freud, "the sexual life of maturing youth is almost entirely restricted to indulging in phantasies, that is, in ideas that are not destined to be carried into effect. In these phantasies the infantile tendencies invariably emerge once more, but this time with intensified pressure from somatic sources." (Freud 1905, 226) Puberty becomes a time of conflict between the demands of genital sexuality and the perverse tendencies that are produced by the re-cathexis of infantile non-genital pleasures. According to Freud, this conflict between adult and infantile sexuality in puberty is at the origin of perversion, neurosis, psychosis and sublimation.[5] In this way, Freud relates our aptitude for psychopathology *and* culture to the specificity of our sexual biology.

By inscribing the possibility of psychopathology into our (sexual) biology, Freud rejects the idea that psychopathology is something accidental to our being human. The sexual perversions, for instance, cannot be considered as pathological aberrations of a supposedly normal sexual instinct. Perverse tendencies are as innate and original as the genital instinct. There is no point in searching for a specific cause of perversion because its "cause" is in human nature as such: "There is indeed something innate lying behind the perversions

---

[4] "Biological changes in sexual life (such as the function's diphasic onset which we have already mentioned, the disappearance of the periodic character of sexual excitation and the transformation in the relation between female menstruation and male excitation)—these innovations in sexuality must have been of high importance in the evolution of animals to man." (Freud 1940, 186) For a recent corroboration of this view, see: Diamond (2002) and Dean et al. (2001). "Our progress from being just another species of big mammal to being uniquely human depended on the remodelling not only of our pelvises and skulls, but also of our sexuality." (Diamond 2002, 57)

[5] "The fact that the onset of sexual development in human beings occurs in two phases, i.e. that the development is interrupted by the period of latency, seemed to call for particular notice. This appears to be one of the necessary conditions of the aptitude of men for developing a higher civilization, but also of their tendency to neurosis." (Freud 1905, 234)

but it is something innate in everyone." (Freud 1905, 171) Since neurosis and psychosis too must be traced back to this specifically human conflict between genital sexuality and the infantile tendencies re-cathected at puberty, all psychopathologies that are specifically human must be considered as *exaggerations* of normal states; not as aberrations from normality: "The neuroses (unlike infectious diseases, for instance) have no specific determinants. It would be idle to seek in them for pathogenic excitants. They shade off by easy transitions into what is described as the normal; and, on the other hand, there is scarcely any state recognized as normal in which indications of neurotic traits could not be pointed out. Neurotics have approximately the same innate dispositions as other people, they have the same experiences and they have the same tasks to perform." (Freud 1940, 183)

Freud's theory of psychopathology thus dismisses the idea that there are experiences or dispositions that can be considered as the specific causes of neurosis. The psychopathology of neurosis, perversion and psychosis cannot be founded on specific aetiologies such as seduction, trauma, or specific organic causes. This does not imply that Freud denies the pathogenic effects of seduction and trauma. But they must be considered as specific problems within a general psychopathology that reveals the structure of human nature as such. For Freud, neurosis, perversion, psychosis[6], and sublimation are the only paradigmatic answers to the universal problem of being a human being. This is the consequence of Freud's radically *dimensional* perspective on psychopathology.[7]

The relation between the pathological and the infantile bridges the gap between pathology and normality because pathology is caused by universally human problems or 'weak points': infantile sexuality and, following our interpretation of the death instinct, the infant's radical *Hilflosigkeit*.[8] In psychoanalysis, therefore, the analysis of the different pathologies has inevitably an anthropological claim. To understand what it means to be human, says Freud, we must analyse the extreme, paradigmatic answers to this problem

---

[6] This anthropological dimension of psychosis was only hinted at by Freud. (Freud 1924) It is Melanie Klein who has shown that the psychotic syndromes of classical psychiatry are merely quantitative exaggerations of "positions" that also determine the mind of normal adults. (Klein 1997)

[7] Peter Fonagy sees this as one of the major contributions psychoanalysis has to offer to attachment theory. According to Fonagy, "the psychoanalytic perspective might encourage us to think less categorically and more dimensionally about attachment security. The potential for both security and insecurity is likely to be present in all of us." (Fonagy 2001, 187)

[8] "If it remains true that the neuroses do not differ in any essential respect from the normal, their study promises to yield us valuable contributions to our knowledge of the normal. It may be that we shall thus discover the 'weak points' in a normal organisation." (Freud 1940, 184)

that we all are ourselves. The analysis of different pathologies will highlight the different aspects of our infantile experience and its *nachträglich* effects. In this perspective, the difference between normality and pathology can only be a quantitative, not a qualitative difference.[9] In this way, *Freud transformed the study of psychopathology into a clinical anthropology*, i.e. a clarification of the specifically human in human nature by analysing its pathological manifestations.

In the following chapters, we will follow Freud in his attempt to understand different psychopathologies as the *nachträglich* effects of infantile sexuality, and we will do so in constant reference to the fact that this relation between the pathological and the infantile is the basis of a clinical anthropology. This historico-structural interpretation of Freud's theory of sexuality will show that the function of sexuality changes radically in the development of his theory. In his earlier theories, sexuality or sexual phantasy is the "traumatic" factor in psychopathology and human nature. In his later theory, sexuality and phantasy are considered more and more as attempts to overcome a more primordial trauma.

---

[9] "*Quantitative* disharmonies are what must be held responsible for the inadequacy and sufferings of neurotics." (Freud 1940, 183)

1. AN INSTINCT PERVERTED BY BEAUTY—*THREE ESSAYS* AS A SEXUAL AESTHETICS

Freud begins his *Three Essays on the Theory of Sexuality* (1905) with an essay on the sexual perversions. In this essay, he depends heavily on the findings of the sexologists of his time. However, "The Sexual Aberrations" must not be read as a mere contribution to sexual psychopathology; indeed, as a phenomenological or aetiological study of the sexual perversions it is rather poor. What is at stake for Freud is not the aetiology of perversion but the nature of sexuality as such. His reference to perversion and sexology is strategic. A confrontation of "The Sexual Aberrations" with Krafft-Ebing's *Psychopathia Sexualis* will highlight the specificity of Freud's understanding of perversion and human sexuality.

According to Freud, human sexuality cannot be reduced to a heterosexual, genital instinct, for in sexuality, we are not primarily interested in the genitals of the other, but in the attractiveness of other parts of the body. Human sexuality, it seems, is essentially "fetishistic". But *why*, then, should the sexual instinct be interested in the aesthetic value of its object? This can only be understood from the perspective of Freud's hypothesis of an organic repression of infantile, non-genital sexuality. This organic repression produces *nachträglich* disgust instead of non-genital sexual excitation. This implies that, in adults, fore-pleasure (kissing, touching, smelling...) has to overcome disgust to become a source of sexual excitation. Freud's hypothesis about the origin of disgust can elucidate the connection between the sexual instinct and beauty. The aesthetic value of the sexual object must be understood as a defence against something repulsive: infantile sexuality.

Instinct and Object

In the first paragraphs of the essay on "The Sexual Aberrations", Freud presents the common idea that sexuality is one biological function among others. There is a sexual instinct as there is an instinct of nutrition, and this sexual instinct has a specific nature determined by its reproductive function. It is characterised by an attraction to the opposite sex, directed towards coitus; it is lacking in childhood and originates at the time of puberty. (Freud 1905, 135) It is well known that this picture of sexuality is destroyed in the *Three Essays*. This destruction has been so thorough that it has led psychoanalysts such as Laplanche (Laplanche 1985, 9) to take a radically anti-biological stance. Sexuality, they say, cannot be considered an instinct because the term "instinct" has the connotation of a pre-established biological function. In line with this argument, they have criticised the English translator of Freud's work, James

Strachey, because he translated *Trieb* as "instinct". It would be preferable, according to them, to translate *Trieb* as "drive" and so to avoid confusion with the German word *Instinkt*. This critique is completely legitimate in view of Freud's deconstruction of sexuality. I think, however, that there are good reasons to maintain Strachey's translation. The first argument is a historical one: At the beginning of the century, biologists and sexologists used the term *Trieb* to denote the biological functions of animals. Thus, when Freud uses the word *Trieb*, this does not imply an anti-biological conception of it. This leads us to a second, theoretical, argument. For Freud, the *Trieb* must be situated at the border between the psychic and the somatic. Therefore, the biological connotation is unavoidable, problematic though it may be. By translating *Trieb* as instinct, this biological connotation is preserved. It must be admitted, however, that this biological connotation does not imply that sexuality is a pre-established, vital *function*. Even from a purely biological perspective, there is something in sexuality that cannot be explained in terms of its function. (Ridley 1993, 130) The biological connotation, however, does emphasise Freud's vision of an endocrinological theory of sexual substances, without which the theory of an *organic* repression and of the *nachträglich* effect of infantile sexuality cannot be maintained. (Freud 1905, 216) This emphasis on the somatic aspect of the instinct, then, highlights the fact that the origin of psycho-sexuality as such is a problem that must be explained. Translating *Trieb* as "drive" avoids Freud's question as to why sexuality is such a peculiar instinct.[1]

Freud begins his essay on "The Sexual Aberrations" with a discussion of homosexuality. Homosexuality shows that the sexual instinct is not characterised by a pre-established, natural attraction to the opposite sex. Freud is not interested, here, in discovering the origin of homosexuality. He only argues that all attempts to explain it (degeneracy (Freud 1905, 138), innateness (Freud 1905, 139), anatomical or neurophysiological bisexuality (Freud 1905, 141), etc.) are unconvincing. What is of interest to Freud, however, is something else. He draws two conclusions from his study of homosexuality:

(1) Homosexuality, and even zoophilia and paedophilia, occur in people who are normal in all other aspects of life. Abnormalities in sexual life cannot be explained by a general mental insanity that would *also* affect sexuality. (Freud 1905, 148)
(2) Homosexuals are abnormal only with regard to their sexual object, not with regard to their sexual aims. Homosexuality does not imply intercourse *per anum*, masturbation, or any other specifically homosexual aim. (Freud 1905, 148)

In these observations Freud is in total agreement with sexologists such as Krafft-Ebing, who says about homosexuality: "The anomaly is limited to the sexual life, and does not more deeply and seriously affect character and mental

---

[1] Compare: Green 1997, 130-133.

personality. The sexual life of these homosexuals, with due alteration of details, is entirely like that in normal hetero-sexual love." (Krafft-Ebing 1997, 275) But only Freud will draw radical conclusions from these observations.

For Krafft-Ebing, homosexuality remains after all a sign of degeneracy. (Krafft-Ebing 1997, 225) In the *Psychopathia Sexualis*, homosexuality is subsumed under the broader category of sexual inversion (*konträre Sexualempfindung*). (Krafft-Ebing 1997, 257) But, what is sexual inversion for Krafft-Ebing is what we today would call transsexualism, which is a question of sexual identity rather than of object-choice. According to Krafft-Ebing, this sexual inversion is a symptom of degeneracy in people who also suffer from other mental or neurotic abnormalities and from other sexual perversions. Homosexuality, then, becomes a subcategory and a mild case of a gender identity disorder. Moreover, Krafft-Ebing's theory of degeneracy implies a strict distinction between normality and pathology, because degeneracy is the cause of pathology. This prevented him from questioning the nature of sexuality as such. The ontological question: "What is sexuality?" remains obscured by the aetiological question: "What is the cause of perversion?"

In the first edition of *Three Essays*, Freud criticises the idea of degeneracy, but he does not develop an alternative aetiology of homosexuality. In opposition to Krafft-Ebing, for whom homosexuality is a subcategory of transsexualism, Freud's conclusions are based only on the observation of homosexuality *stricto sensu*.[2] Freud distinguishes homosexuality in a strict sense from inversion (*konträre Sexualempfindung*) because, with regard to homosexuality, he has a strong case against degeneracy. Homosexuals are normal people. Their sexual life is approximately the same as that of heterosexuals. Therefore, homosexuality is not the symptom of a morbid personality, but a "symptom" of sexuality itself. For Freud, the existence of homosexuality puts the nature of sexuality as such into question. It shows us that the link between the instinct and the object has become a riddle. (Freud 1905, 148)

The loosening of the bond between the sexual instinct and its natural object does not mean, however, that *in concreto* the sexual object is unimportant. It is true that the sexual instinct is not, by nature, aimed at a person of the opposite sex. But, then, a new question arises: What is the object of the untameable attraction that is so characteristic of sexuality? According to Krafft-Ebing, a certain amount of *fetishism* is essential to any kind of love. Certain parts of the body, such as the hair, the hands, the smell, the gaze or the voice, are especially suited for this normal or "physiological" fetishism. In fashion and cos-

---

[2] In 1985, Robert Stoller still has to remind psychoanalysts of this distinction: "Analysts, like less educated folk, sometimes confuse these gender (masculine/feminine) attributes with erotic issues when judging homosexuality, in the inaccurate belief that visible cross-gender impulses inevitably signal homosexual erotic choice, even if the latter is not consciously experienced." (Stoller 1985, 98)

metics, women make these parts of their bodies the object of special care. Krafft-Ebing says: "Woman certainly seems to be more or less conscious of these facts. For she devotes great attention to her hair and often spends an unreasonable amount of time and money upon its cultivation." (Krafft-Ebing 1997, 19) The function of fashion is to highlight the looks and so to attract the sexual interest of others by emphasising certain parts of the body. Love is impossible, according to Krafft-Ebing, where there is no attraction to a part of the body that makes an impression that it does not deserve in itself. Even when love is experienced as a pure "harmony of souls", it can be traced back to the attraction by a certain part of the body and, thus, to sexual attraction. (Krafft-Ebing 1997, 16) This fascination for a part of the other's body has two important functions in sexual life. First, it makes love blind: the attraction to a certain part of the body neutralises the unattractive aspects of the object. Second, it makes love concrete and individual. Thanks to this normal fetishism, what is sexually stimulating for one person may be ridiculously personal and incomprehensible to others. (Krafft-Ebing 1997, 17) This description of normal fetishism implies that, even for Krafft-Ebing, sexual attraction to another person is ultimately based on the attraction of the sexual instinct to *a non-genital part* of the other's body, not to the genitals.

For Krafft-Ebing, a certain amount of fetishism is essential to sexuality, but this insight does not persuade him to question sexuality as such, nor to re-think the relation between sexual normality and perversion. For Freud, on the other hand, the attraction by non-genital parts of the other's body is the keystone for a new perspective on the nature of sexuality. The sexual instinct is not directed by nature to an object of the opposite sex, but this does not mean that in someone's concrete sexual life anything can be a sexual object. What determines the sexual instinct at the level of the object is not the other's sex, but something *about* the other. Even the most vulgar lover is interested in the *looks* of the sexual object, not (only) in the genitals: "It is only in the rarest instances that the psychical valuation that is set on the sexual object, as being the goal of the sexual instinct, stops short at its genitals. The appreciation extends to the whole body of the sexual object and tends to involve every sensation derived from it" (Freud 1905, 150). According to Freud, this "overvaluation of the sexual object" is essential to human sexuality. Freud's concept of sexual overvaluation introduces the *fetishistic* dimension of human sexuality. This implies that what is overvaluated in sexual overvaluation is the sexual significance of non-genital parts of the other's body, not the other as such.

In a footnote to the *Three Essays* which was added in 1910, Freud says that although the experience of beauty is rooted in sexual excitation, "[W]e never regard the genitals themselves, the sight of which produces the strongest sexual excitation, as really 'beautiful'." (Freud 1905, 156) Thus, sexual overvaluation implies that the sexual instinct is always already deflected by beauty, away from a direct interest in the genitals of the other. The importance of the beauty and the looks of the sexual object highlight the fact that even heterosexual, genital sexuality is essentially characterised by a *detour* on its way to the genitals of the other. This deflection of the sexual instinct, says Freud, is supported by culture. The parts of the other's body which produce the most sexual excitation (the genitals), are covered by clothing. But the concealment of the body at the same time arouses sexual curiosity. (Freud 1905, 156) Sexuality is thus directed towards the genitals, but this directedness is aroused *and* deflected by the beauty of other parts of the body. Freud, here, radicalises the importance of Krafft-Ebing's "physiological fetishism". The detour through the non-genital parts of the body is not just a frivolity of nature, but the structure of sexuality itself. It is supported, not just by fashion (*Mode / Koketterie*) (Krafft-Ebing 1997, 15), but by civilisation (*Kultur*). (Freud 1905, 156)

Apparently, the sexual instinct is attracted to beauty, and thus to non-genital parts of the other's body, since the genitals are never regarded "as really 'beautiful'." (Freud 1905, 156) From reading the *Three Essays*, however, it does not become clear *why* the sexual instinct is characterised by this detour through beauty. If the sight of the genitals produces the strongest sexual excitation, why is the sexual instinct only *indirectly* aimed at the genitals of the other? According to Freud, the original meaning of "beautiful" was "sexually stimulating." (Freud 1905, 156) But he never clarifies what constitutes the specific *difference* between beauty and its origin (sexual excitation). He only observes that the sexual instinct is characterised by an interest in beautiful parts of the other's body, and only indirectly by an interest in the genitals. This implies that, in sexuality, the pleasure principle appears to be modified by a "principle of aesthetic modesty" from the start. (Nancy 1993, 230) But *why* does the sexual instinct care about beauty? Freud only observes it as a fact, but, in the *Three Essays*, he does not *explain* how it comes about that the sexual instinct has "taste".

Overcoming Disgust

"A man who will kiss a pretty girl's lips passionately, may perhaps be disgusted at the idea of using her toothbrush, though there are no grounds for supposing that his own oral cavity, for which he feels no disgust, is any cleaner than the girl's." (Freud 1905, 151-152) Apparently, the pleasure experienced in kissing presupposes an overriding of disgust. Freud's example reveals the true meaning of the sexual overvaluation of the object. Kissing produces pleasure only when the girl is pretty. Otherwise, it would produce disgust. Freud's notion of sexual overvaluation is the radicalisation of Krafft-Ebing's "normal fetishism". According to Krafft-Ebing, "love exhibits itself (…) as a profound anomaly which attains what seemed impossible, *renders the ugly beautiful*, the profane sublime." (Krafft-Ebing 1997, 17, my emphasis). For Krafft-Ebing, this "anomaly" remains an unnecessary surplus to the genital sexual instinct.

For Freud, on the other hand, rendering the ugly beautiful is essential to human sexuality because the normal reaction to the mouth and the anus of the other is one of disgust. However, sexual overvaluation can override this disgust and thus make non-genital fore-pleasure possible. (Freud 1905, 152) Freud also emphasises that the genitals do not provoke disgust, but that equally they are not considered beautiful either. (Freud 1905, 152) This is a first indication that beauty is the exact reverse of disgust. Normally, beauty and disgust are limited to *non-genital* sexuality.

In "The Sexual Aberrations", however, Freud does not analyse the fact that the non-genital parts of the other's body provoke disgust. Therefore, the problem of what motivates the sexual overvaluation of the object, "which renders the ugly beautiful", remains obscure. In a letter to W. Fliess of November 14, 1897, however, Freud had proposed a hypothesis about the origin of disgust, and it is only in the context of this hypothesis that Freud's emphasis on sexual overvaluation becomes intelligible. According to this letter, disgust is an effect of the organic repression of an infantile, non-genital pleasure.[3] (Freud 1985, 279) This means that in infancy, the mouth and the anus were erotogenic zones, which were later abandoned. This abandonment of the oral and anal erotogenic zones, says Freud, is the phylogenetic heritage of man's adoption of an erect posture, which resulted in the depreciation of his sense of smell. (Freud 1909, 248) Without this normal sexual repression, we would remain in a state of *originäre Verrücktheit* (originary madness). (Freud 1986, 429) When the memory traces of infantile pleasures are re-activated after the abandoning of the erotogenic zones, this generates disgust instead of sexual excitation. Freud discovered this fact—that disgust has its origin in a repressed memory of an earlier pleasure—in his analyses of hysterical patients. The introduction of a *normal* sexual repression, however, implies that the same mechanism underlies normal disgust. This analysis of disgust can elucidate Freud's insistence on sexual overvaluation as an essential characteristic of human sexuality. Apparently, human sexuality is essentially "fetishistic" *because* it has to overcome a disgust of infantile sexuality.

To understand the relation between sexual overvaluation and disgust, we must understand the psycho-dynamics of fetishism. In the first edition of the *Three Essays* (1905), Freud introduces sexual overvaluation and fetishism, but he does not explain what motivates this "normal fetishism" of human sexuality. The footnotes added in 1910, however, elucidate Freud's understanding of

---

[3] In *Three Essays*, Freud briefly mentions this idea of an organic repression of infantile sexuality, but he does not explain it as an abandoning of the erotogenic zones owing to the loss of smell as a source of sexual excitation: "One gets an impression from civilized children that the construction of these dams is a product of education, and no doubt education has much to do with it. But in reality this development is organically determined and fixed by heredity, and it can occasionally occur without any help at all from education." (Freud 1905, 177-8)

fetishism and sexual overvaluation. In 1910, after the publication of *Notes upon a Case of Obsessional Neurosis* (Freud 1909, 248) and after his correspondence with Karl Abraham on a case of foot-fetishism, Freud re-introduces his hypothesis about an organic repression of the pleasure in smell. Freud says that "in the perversion that corresponds to foot-fetishism, it is only dirty and evil-smelling feet that become sexual objects." (Freud 1905, 155) As such, however, this is not true. Not every foot-fetishist is sexually excited by dirty feet. In his article, *Remarks on the Psycho-analysis of a Case of Foot and Corset Fetishism*, Abraham reports the analysis of a patient whose exclusive sexual interest was in beautiful, elegant shoes, while "ugly shoes repelled me and filled me with feelings of disgust." (Abraham 1949, 126) According to Abraham, "the particular need felt by the fetishist for aesthetic value in his sexual object indicates that his libido *originally* sought certain aims which seem particularly unaesthetic to the generality of normal adults and give rise to feelings of disgust in them." (Abraham 1949, 129) Abraham's analysis implies that Freud's reference to dirty and evil-smelling feet must be understood differently. In a letter to Abraham, Freud says: "I have learnt from other cases that shoe-fetishism goes back to an *original* (olfactory) pleasure in the dirty and stinking foot." (Freud/Abraham 1965, 87, my emphasis) Dirty feet are not as such the sexual objects of a foot-fetishist. He is aroused by beautiful shoes because, as a child, he obtained pleasure from smelling dirty feet. This pleasure, then, succumbed to repression. To regain his infantile pleasure, he must make a detour through the beautiful, elegant shoes. So, the infantile pleasure in odours that, owing to organic repression, will become disgusting afterwards, is the "original", infantile factor in fetishism. This infantile pleasure in what will later become disgusting motivates the need for aesthetic value. The fetish has a double function. On the one hand, it enables the return to an infantile pleasure; while on the other hand, the aesthetic value of the object prevents a reaction of disgust. This brief excursion into the dynamics of fetishism, then, solves the riddle of why the sexual instinct takes an interest in beauty. Without sexual overvaluation of the object ("aesthetic value"), a reproduction of infantile pleasure would generate disgust instead of pleasure.

Scopophilia and Beauty

Looking plays an important part in human sexuality. In voyeurism, it even becomes the dominant sexual activity. Abraham's patient is aroused by *looking* at elegant shoes. The analysis of his foot-fetishism reveals a change, not only from dirty feet to elegant shoes, but also from smelling to looking. Apparently, the repression of the pleasure in smell led to a transformation of the sexual aim. The importance of beauty for human sexuality, it seems, can only be understood from the perspective of this transformation from smelling to looking.

In Krafft-Ebing's *Psychopathia sexualis*, only one paragraph deals with voyeurism. According to Krafft-Ebing, voyeurs are "men who are so cynical that they seek to get sight of coitus, in order to assist their virility; or who seek to have orgasm and ejaculation at the sight of an excited woman." (Krafft-Ebing 1997, 390) This definition of voyeurism is a very limited one. Krafft-Ebing does not take into account that looking plays an important part in normal sexuality or that normal people as well as voyeurs are sexually excited by the sight of an excited woman. This limited perspective upon voyeurism, however, is not due to narrow-mindedness. It is a consequence of his theory of perversion. Krafft-Ebing makes a radical distinction between perversion and perversity. Perversities are perverse *acts*. The diagnosis of perversion, however, does not depend upon acts, but upon the personality and the motives of the one who performs these acts. According to Krafft-Ebing, "perversion of the sexual instinct... is not to be confounded with perversity in the sexual act; since the latter may be induced by conditions other than psycho-pathological. The concrete perverse act, monstrous as it may be, is clinically not decisive. In order to differentiate between disease (perversion) and vice (perversity), one must investigate the whole personality of the individual and the original motive leading to the perverse act." (Krafft-Ebing 1997, 68) This distinction between perversion and perversity implies at the same time a radical break between normal sexuality and sexual pathology. Normal people can perform perverse acts. But this does not imply a perversion of the sexual instinct. According to Krafft-Ebing, the diagnosis of perversion depends upon "the whole personality of the individual", not on the perverse character of certain sexual acts. Freud, however, emphasises that the sexual instinct is relatively independent from the personality of the individual. People who are normal in all other aspects of life can be "sick persons in the single sphere of sexual life." (Freud 1905, 161) Therefore, Krafft-Ebing's criterion of "the whole personality" cannot be decisive in matters of sexuality. Freud goes even further. He says that "manifest abnormality in the other relations of life can invariably be shown to have a background of abnormal sexual conduct." (Freud 1905, 161) This implies that the whole of psychopathology, sexual or otherwise, must be considered as having a sexual aetiology. (Freud 1905, 165) The whole personality of the individual, including both his sexual life and his other relations, must be understood from the perspective of sexuality. According to Freud, sexuality may influence the whole personality, but not the other way around. Perversions cannot be the symptoms of a "personality". (Freud 1905, 148) Otherwise, it would be impossible for a normal person to have an abnormal sexual life. Therefore, the distinction between perversion of the sexual instinct and perversity of the sexual act becomes insignificant for Freud. The sexual perversions must be considered as the original constituents of the sexual instinct because they have no "cause" outside of sexuality, such as degeneracy of the personality. (Freud 1905, 171) This means that looking as fore-pleasure in normal sexuality is not qualitatively different from voyeurism as sexual pathology. (Freud 1905, 149) Freud, therefore, emphasises the fact that "visual impressions remain the most frequent pathway along which libidinal excitation is aroused," and that there is no essential difference between this and voyeurism. (Freud 1905, 156)

According to Freud, every non-genital sexual activity has to overcome a force that opposes it. Disgust, which opposes the extension of the sexual interest to non-genital parts of the other's body, is such a force. The force that opposes voyeurism, says Freud, is shame. (Freud 1905, 157) But here, again, he cannot explain how this comes about, because, in the *Three Essays*, he does not analyse the origin of the sense of shame. Our interpretation of sexual overvaluation as an overcoming of disgust, however, can elucidate the dynamic relation of voyeurism and shame. Abraham's patient, who once was aroused by the smell of dirty feet, has become a shoe-fetishist. This means, however, that now he is sexually excited by *looking* at elegant shoes. Looking has taken over the sexual significance of smell. His fetishism involves not only a transition from dirty feet to elegant shoes, but also a transformation of the sexual *aim*: from smelling to looking. This transformation is not analysed in the *Three Essays*, but in his clinical observations Freud stresses the transformation of the sexual aim from smell to looking in fetishism. In his correspondence with Abraham, he describes one of his patients—a fetishist—as follows: "His childhood was full of unusually intense coprophilic activity.... In the years of puberty he was a voyeur, and his masturbation began with his spying on some American girls undressing in a Swiss hotel." (Freud/Abraham 1965, 87) About another fetishist, he remarks: "It is true that the urge to smell plays no role in his case; it may be that this urge was replaced by voyeurism." (Freud 1975, 246) It is clear from these quotes that Freud considered voyeurism as a *transformed* sexual aim. This is in line with Freud's hypothesis of an organic repression of the erogenicity of the smell. According to this hypothesis, the re-activation of memory traces connected to the smell produces disgust. As such, however, this says nothing about the relation between voyeurism and shame. But in his letter to Fliess of November 14, 1897, Freud says that disgust is "the affective basis" for shame (Freud 1985, 280). Freud does not elucidate the relation of disgust to shame, but Abraham's analysis of foot-fetishism shows that the transition from disgust to shame depends upon the transformation of the sexual aim from smelling to looking. After the organic repression of pleasure in smell and the emergence of disgust, looking substitutes for smell as the dominant source of sexual excitation. It is this transformation of the sexual aim that accounts for the change in the form of resistance from disgust to shame. Only this hypothesis of a transformation of the sexual aim can explain Freud's idea that disgust is the affective basis for shame, and that every sexual aim has its own form of resistance. Shame is to looking what disgust is to smelling.

This transformation of the sexual aim (from smelling to looking) also accounts for the role of beauty in human sexuality. Beauty is primarily visual. The excitations produced by touching and smelling do not generate an experience of beauty *stricto sensu*. Beauty is in the *eye* of the beholder. According to

Freud, "[T]he eye is perhaps the zone most remote from the sexual object, but it is the one which, in the situation of wooing an object, is liable to be the most frequently stimulated by the particular quality of excitation whose cause, when it occurs in a sexual object, we describe as beauty." (Freud 1905, 209) The importance of beauty in sexuality is linked to the sexual significance of looking, and as such it is a consequence of the transformation of the sexual aim from smelling to looking. There are beautiful looks, but there are no "beautiful" smells.[4]

This insight into the relation between beauty and the transformation of the sexual aim can solve our problem as to *why and how* the sexual instinct is dominated by a "principle of aesthetic modesty". (Nancy 1993, 230) The sexual instinct takes an interest in beauty because it has to overcome disgust. Disgust can be overcome by beauty when looking has substituted for smell as the predominant sexual aim. Abraham's patient is aroused by *looking* at *elegant* shoes. He is disgusted, however, when he sees dirty shoes. Seeing dirty shoes brings him in too close a contact with the original pleasure in smelling dirty feet, which now, after organic repression, provokes disgust instead of libido. Looking at elegant shoes defends him against a too direct confrontation with this original infantile pleasure.

Conclusion

Three Essays on the Theory of Sexuality (1905) is a synthesis of Freud's ideas about human sexuality. Before Freud, sexologists such as Krafft-Ebing, Moll, Hirschfeld, and others already studied the sexual perversions. In the *Three Essays*, Freud depends heavily upon the work of these sexologists. However, *Three Essays* has a much more radical claim than the studies of sexual psychopathology of Freud's time. According to Freud, the sexual perversions cannot be understood as aberrations of the normal sexual instinct. They are, on the contrary, its original constituents. Freud's introduction of infantile sexuality destroyed the essential difference between normal sexuality and sexual perversion. The sexual perversions only show in an exaggerated form the origin and the nature of *human* sexuality as such. What is specifically human in human sexuality can only be understood from the perspective of sexual psychopathology. This anthropological claim is essential to Freud's theory of sexuality in *Three Essays*. Freud's analysis of "normal fetishism" reveals how fetishism and voyeurism constitute the aesthetic dimension of human sexuality, and how this aesthetic dimension can overcome the repulsive effects of infantile sexuality.

---

[4] Even perfumes are not beautiful *stricto sensu*, but they can be seductive. Freud's hypothesis of an organic repression of pleasure in smell can explain the fact that in the case of perfumes there is always a thin line between what is seductive and what is repulsive.

2. What is Sexual about Infantile "Sexuality"?

In the previous chapter, we have seen how Freud analysed perversion as a search for an original infantile pleasure. This search demands an overpowering of disgust and shame because these infantile pleasures are abandoned after repression, and the re-activation of their memory traces generates unpleasure instead of pleasure. But the transformation of the sexual aim from smelling to looking produces an "aesthetic modesty" which enables a modified re-finding of the original pleasure. In this chapter, we will discuss Freud's idea that this 'original infantile pleasure' is already a *sexual* pleasure in its own right. What does this mean?

The sexual perversions show that sexuality is broader than genital sexuality. Voyeurism, fetishism and sadomasochism are indeed sexual aims, which can become independent of any interest in genital sexuality. Fetishists, for instance, are not interested in the genitals of the other. Some perverts do not even describe their own sexual excitation as a genital excitation. Abraham's patient "had a strong antipathy to manual self-gratification." Instead, he felt an "inward joy" at the sight of dainty shoes.[1] This non-genital sexuality also plays an important part in the fore-pleasures of normal sexuality. Apparently, (normal and perverse) adult sexuality is not just aimed at coitus and orgasm. Everything in adult sexuality, apart from coitus and orgasm, is dominated by the unconscious memories of infantile, non-genital pleasures. But is this enough to justify Freud's claim that these infantile pleasures were therefore already sexual? For adults, *fellatio* is a sexual activity in which the memory traces of infantile oral pleasure are re-activated. Does this mean, however, that sucking the mother's breast or thumb-sucking is a sexual activity for the child? Is non-genital pleasure perverse sexuality? According to Freud, "children behave in the same kind of way as an average uncultivated woman in whom the same polymorphously perverse disposition persists." (Freud 1905, 191) In the adult sexuality of Freud's "uncultivated woman", however, oral and anal pleasures are preliminary to, or substituted for, genital pleasure. This is not the case for the child. But given that, it is hard to understand why the oral and anal pleasures of the child must be considered as infantile *perverse sexuality*. In this chapter, I will argue that Freud has only biological arguments to determine the sexual character of pre-genital sexuality. Darwin, Haeckel and Fliess had already broadened the concept of sexuality beyond the limits of genitality, and this reference to biology is crucial for understanding Freud's theory of sexuality.

---

[1] Abraham 1949, 126. See also "modern" perversions such as "nursing" and "feeding".

A Pleasure beyond Satisfaction

According to Freud, thumb-sucking is an infantile *sexual* activity. (Freud 1905, 179) But what are his arguments for this broadening of the concept of sexuality? In thumb-sucking, says Freud, the child repeats an older pleasure: sucking the mother's breast for milk. In sucking the mother's breast, the child satisfies his hunger. At the same time, however, the sucking produces a surplus of pleasure. The infant not only satisfies his hunger, he also finds pleasure in doing so. But the search for milk and the search for pleasure do not share the same destiny.[2] The search for milk eventually ends in the satisfaction of the need. The search for pleasure, on the other hand, has no such natural end. In *Jokes and their Relation to the Unconscious* (1905), Freud says, "If we do not require our mental apparatus at the moment for supplying one of our indispensable satisfactions, we allow it itself to work in the direction of pleasure and we seek to derive pleasure from its own activity." (Freud 1905, 95) Applied to the infant sucking the mother's breast, this means that the pleasure of sucking continues after the need for milk is satisfied. In thumb-sucking, there is obviously no satisfaction of hunger anymore.[3] Thumb-sucking, then, reveals this pleasure beyond satisfaction that was already implicitly present in sucking the mother's breast. In thumb-sucking or in anal masturbation, the search for pleasure has become independent from the vital functions that originally generated this pleasure. According to Freud, this detachment of pleasure from satisfaction enables all vital activities of the child to become autoerotic. "Autoerotic" refers to the fact that the infant finds pleasure in the manipulation of the erotogenic zones of his own body and that this pleasure has become detached from the object of the *vital* function. What is crucial to Freud's notion of autoerotism is the idea that autoerotic activities reveal the fact that the search for pleasure does not end with the satisfaction of the need. Thumb-sucking as an autoerotic activity indicates that sucking the mother's breast for milk generates a pleasure beyond the need for milk.[4]

---

[2] "The satisfaction of the erotogenic zone is associated, in the first instance, with the satisfaction of the need for nourishment. To begin with, sexual activity attaches itself to one of the functions serving the purpose of self-preservation and does not become independent from them until later." (Freud 1905, 182)

[3] "There is no question of the purpose of this procedure being the taking of nourishment." (Freud 1905, 180)

[4] But this does not imply that the search for pleasure has another, phantasmatic object, as Laplanche says in *Life and Death in Psychoanalysis*: "Autoerotism, it will be remembered, was, as early as 1905, posited not as a primal, objectless state of the human being, but as the result of a double, integrated movement: a turning away from functional activities which, initially, were oriented towards a certain objectality, an "object-value"; and a turning around of the activity on itself, *in the direction of phantasy*." (Laplanche 1985, 72, my emphasis) According to our interpretation, there is no indication that Freud considered autoerotism as phantasmatic in the *Three Essays*.

For Freud, this difference between pleasure and the satisfaction of needs justifies the qualification of thumb-sucking as a sexual activity. Obviously, thumb-sucking is not in the service of self-preservation and, therefore, it can only be a sexual activity. According to Freud, "the baby's obstinate persistence in sucking gives evidence at an early stage of a need for satisfaction which, though it originates from and is instigated by the taking of nourishment, nevertheless strives to obtain pleasure independently of nourishment and *for that reason* may and should be termed sexual." (Freud 1940, 154, my emphasis) Of course, this argument is only intelligible within the framework of a dualistic theory of the instincts; according to Freud, there are only two fundamental instincts: self-preservation and sexuality.[5]

A Reference to Biology

This dualistic theory of the instincts is not an invention of Freud. It is one of the fundamental discoveries of evolutionary biology. Ernst Haeckel, a biologist and philosopher who introduced Darwinism in the German world, laid great stress on the philosophical implications of Darwin's theory. According to Haeckel, Darwinism implies that Nature is one. This means that everything that is considered spiritual or cultural is nevertheless a part of nature, dominated by the same laws.[6] Within nature, however, there are *two* fundamental "agents": natural and sexual selection. Even for Darwin, it was clear that not everything could be explained by natural selection. Especially human nature, which includes human culture, shows a lot of characteristics that must appear frivolous from the perspective of adaptation and simple reproduction. According to Darwin, everything that is useless for survival and adaptation to the daily habits of life can only be the result of sexual selection. (Darwin 1989, 597)

Darwin's most notorious example of sexual selection is the peacock's tail. The long, beautiful tail of the peacock, Darwin acknowledged, cannot be the result of natural selection. It is rather a threat to the survival of the peacock.[7]

---

[5] In his book, *Evolution and Individual Behaviour, An Introduction to Human Sociobiology*, Christopher Badcock says, "Freud interpreted what today we would call *oral behaviour* as something to do with sex because he correctly recognized its essential nature: what we may define as *compulsive sucking independent of immediate hunger*." (Badcock 1991, 223) Apparently, it takes an evolutionary biologist to take Freud's identification of "pleasure beyond need" with "sexuality" for granted.

[6] For a detailed history of the influence of Darwinism on Freud, see: Ritvo (1990) and Assoun (1981, 189-216).

[7] Ridley says, "Gaudy males seemed a peculiar result of natural selection since it was hard to imagine that gaudiness helped the animal to survive." (Ridley 1993, 130)

Still, the tail must be the result of selection. In a gesture that resembles Freud's, Darwin comes to the conclusion that the tail can only be the result of *sexual* selection. The peahen seems to choose a mate on the basis of a taste for beauty.[8] But Darwin could not answer the question of why this was the case. He only observed that this element of taste could not be reduced to natural selection. Some Neo-Darwinists hold the view that the peahen chooses the peacock with the longest, most beautiful tail to mate, not to have the fittest, healthiest offspring, but to have "sexy sons", whose charms will attract the attention of future females.[9] Darwin did not hold this view. For him, aesthetic taste is a strange, "unnatural" element in nature. According to Darwin, tastes are not inherited because otherwise there would exist an ideal standard of beauty. Aesthetic taste, however, is a peculiar liking for variety and moderate extremes. At least in human beings, therefore, taste does not judge according to a standard. This means that, although the sexy characteristics are inherited, the taste for it is not.[10] Therefore, what is sexually selected is the weak spot in evolution, because it depends upon the taste of the other sex, and not on the adaptation to the necessities of life. The example of the peacock's tail shows that sexual selection can threaten adaptation and survival,[11] because the tail is only there to impress the girls.

This sexual selection plays a major role in the evolution of man. The most distinctive features of human nature are the result of sexual selection. According to Darwin, our mental powers and language are not the result of natural

---

[8] "In species where the females get nothing useful from their mates, they seem to choose on aesthetic criteria alone." (Ridley 1993, 130)

[9] "The question Darwin failed to answer was: why? Why on earth should females prefer gaudiness in males?... Once most females are choosing to mate with some males rather than others and are using tail length as the criterion... then any female who bucks the trend and chooses a short-tailed male will have short-tailed sons. Yet all the other females are looking for long-tailed males, so those short-tailed sons will not have much success." (Ridley 1993, 135)

[10] Concerning human beings, Darwin says, "The senses of man and of the lower animals seem to be so constituted that brilliant colours and certain forms, as well as harmonious and rhythmical sounds, give pleasure and are called beautiful; but why this should be so, we know not. It is certainly not true that there is in the mind of man any universal standard of beauty with respect to the human body. It is, however, possible that certain tastes may in the course of time become inherited, though there is no evidence in favour of this belief; and if so, each race would possess its own innate ideal standard of beauty. It has been argued that ugliness consists in an approach to the structure of the lower animals, and no doubt this is partly true with the more civilised nations, in which intellect is highly appreciated; but this explanation will hardly apply to all forms of ugliness. The men of each race prefer what they are accustomed to; they cannot endure any great change; but they like variety, and admire each characteristic carried to a moderate extreme." (Darwin 1989, 607-8)

[11] "This female preference for male ornaments can actually be a threat to the survival of the males." (Ridley 1993, 134)

selection alone; they are acquired partly through the play of charm and seduction between the sexes. Language developed out of music.[12] Music, in its turn, is the result of sexual selection. According to Darwin, poetry is our "most mysterious" capacity because "neither the enjoyment nor the capacity of producing musical notes are faculties of the least use to man in reference to his daily habits of life." (Darwin 1989, 593)[13] The same goes for tattoos, fancy clothes, body-painting, etc. (Darwin 1989, 596-608) What is useless with regard to self-preservation (natural selection) can only have its origin in the taste of the opposite sex (sexual selection).[14] Darwin says, "The impassioned orator, bard, or musician, when with varied tones and cadences he excites the strongest emotions in his hearers, little suspects that he uses the same means by which his half-human ancestors long ago roused each other's ardent passions, during courtship and rivalry." (Darwin 1989, 596) Darwin's theory reveals a fundamental dualism in nature. Two laws determine our destiny: the *Not des Lebens* and the taste of the other sex. According to Haeckel, the fundamental achievements of human culture, such as the family and the state, but also perversion and crime, must be ascribed to the effects of sexual selection.[15] In Freud's time, these ideas were common among biologists and sexologists. Krafft-Ebing, for instance, says in the introduction to his *Psychopathia sexualis* that religion, ethics and art depend upon the sexual instinct (Krafft-Ebing 1997, 2). Of course, such ideas can only be understood from the perspective of

---

[12] "Musical sounds afforded one of the bases for the development of language." (Darwin 1989, 596)

[13] Apparently, contemporary evolutionary psychology forgot about Darwin's explanation of music in terms of sexual selection. Therefore, Pinker cannot understand the evolutionary basis of music: "Music is an enigma... What benefit could there be to diverting time and energy to the making of plinking noises, or to feel sad when no one has died?... As far as biological cause and effect are concerned, music is useless. It shows no signs of design for attaining a goal such as long life, grandchildren, or the accurate perception and prediction of the world." (Pinker 1998, 528) For Krafft-Ebing, the "usefulness" of music was not an enigma: "Singers of renown easily touch woman's heart. They are overwhelmed with love letters and offers of marriage. Tenors have a decided advantage." (Krafft-Ebing 1997, 15)

[14] "An English philosopher goes so far as to maintain that clothes were first made for ornament and not for warmth." (Darwin 1989, 597) It is thus even impossible to decide what is the effect of natural and what of sexual selection.

[15] „Sind nicht so viele andere berühmte Dichtungen bloss der poetische Ausdruck des unermessliche Einflusses, welchen die Liebe und die davon abhängige "sexuelle Selektion" seit der Differenzierung der beiden Geschlechter auf den Gang der Weltgeschichte ausgeübt hat?... Wir verehren in ihr den mächtigsten Faktor der menslichen Gesittung, die Grundlage des Familienlebens und dadurch der Staatsentwicklung. Auf der anderen Seite fürchten wir in ihr die verzehrende Flamme, welche den Unglücklichen in das Verderben treibt, und welche mehr Elend, Laster und Verbrechen verursacht hat, als alle anderen Uebel des Menschengeschlechts zusammengenommen." (Haeckel 1910, 875, my emphasis).

evolutionary biology and its distinction between natural and sexual selection. Everything that is not dominated by the necessities of life resulted from the taste of the other sex.

In this way, Darwinism presents a new conception of what is "sexual". It follows from Darwin's idea of sexual selection that "sexual" is not opposed to "non-genital", but to "natural". According to this view, the reproductive function as such is "natural" (the result of natural selection), while "sexual" must be understood as "un-natural". "Sexual" thus indicates everything that is superfluous from the perspective of natural selection. It is no wonder that after Darwin perversion becomes the anthropological question *par excellence*. What cannot be explained in terms of adaptation must be explained in terms of seduction. This reveals the importance of Krafft-Ebing's notion of physiological fetishism, which is just another word for Darwin's sexual selection.[16] The sexual instinct makes a detour on the way to its (reproductive) function. When Freud radicalised this idea of normal fetishism, sexuality became the key to the understanding of what is specifically human in human nature.

This short reference to Darwinism shows that Freud's dualism of self-preservation and sexuality, and the shift in the concept of sexuality it implies, must be understood from the perspective of evolutionary biology. According to Freud, everything that exceeds the sphere of self-preservation must be considered sexual. A pleasure beyond the satisfaction of vital needs is *therefore* a sexual pleasure. This dualism is as fundamental to Darwinism as it is to psychoanalysis.

Sexual Chemistry

Darwinism, however, did not thematise the sexual character of *infantile* pleasure. It was rather Wilhelm Fliess who took this step. Especially in psychoanalytic literature, Fliess's work and its influence on Freud have been minimised;[17] and Fliess's ideas have been dismissed as delusions. For Freud, on the other hand, Fliess's sexual biology was to be the biological basis of psychoanalytic theory.[18]

In *Die Beziehungen zwischen Nase und weiblichen Geschlechtsorganen* (1897), Fliess argues that the menstrual cycle influences the occurrence of nose-bleeding, illnesses, anxiety-attacks, etc. in women (Fliess 1977, 238). This led Fliess to the hypothesis that there exist sexual substances that influence

---

[16] Even their examples are identical: beards, fashion, the voice, the song of birds, etc.
[17] See, for example, Gay 1989, 56. For a more sympathetic and correct view of Fliess, see: Sulloway (1979).
[18] Freud calls Fliess's sexual biology the organic foundation (*die Organgrundlage*) and his own theories the superstructure (*der Oberbau*). (Freud 1986, 221)

different physiological processes in the woman's body, and not just the sexual organs. This hypothesis was corroborated later by the discovery of the sexual hormones. But what is important for the idea of infantile sexuality is the fact that, according to Fliess, the menstrual cycle is transferred from the mother to the child, including the *male* child. (Fliess 1977, 14) In this way, the sexual substances have a decisive influence on our lives from our conception to our death, and not just from puberty to menopause. This idea of transference from the mother to the infant establishes the existence of infantile sexuality.

According to Fliess, the same substance that causes sexual desire in the sexually mature man supports the development of the organism in the child and advances the decay of the organism after puberty. (Fliess 1977, 238) The development of the teeth, enuresis, and the *pavor noctis* of children are some of the phenomena that depend upon the sexual substances. Fliess was also the first to publish the idea that thumb-sucking is a sexual activity (Fliess 1977, 221-2).[19] How Fliess elaborated these findings into a general sexual biology is not important for our purpose. The point is that his proto-endocrinology broadened the scope of sexuality beyond what is sexual from a phenomenological perspective. According to Fliess, the sexual character of infantile pleasures is determined by the fact that these pleasures are generated by sexual substances. Therefore, only biology can determine what is sexual about infantile sexuality.

In the first edition of the *Three Essays* (1905), Freud already states that his dualistic theory of the instincts will have to be based on endocrinological findings. These findings will reveal "that there is a special chemistry of the sexual function." (Freud 1905, 219) It is true that Freud was not interested in the concrete elaborations of endocrinology. For Freud, any theory would do "provided that its fundamental nature remained unchanged—that is, the emphasis which it lays upon sexual chemistry." (Freud 1905, 216) What is sexual about infantile sexuality, then, becomes a matter of chemistry. Freud and Fliess were especially interested in the role of the thyroid gland in the production of sexual excitation, because this implies that "the puberty-gland is not the only organ concerned with the production of sexual excitation and sexual characters." (Freud 1905, 215, see also: Fliess 1977, 275) In his book of 1897, Fliess anticipated Freud's later idea that sexual chemistry broadens the scope of sexuality beyond genitality: "Some organs that are ordinarily not regarded as sexual are related to each other and to sexuality." (Fliess 1977, 278, my translation) For Freud, these endocrinological facts must be considered the organic basis of the erotogenicity of the erotogenic zones.[20]

---

[19] In the *Three Essays*, Freud refers to Lindner, but not to Fliess. However, Fliess's book was published the same year as Lindner's article on thumb-sucking (1897).

[20] "It seems probable, then, that special chemical substances are produced in the interstitial portion of the sex-glands; these are then taken up in the blood stream and cause particular parts of the central nervous system to be charged with sexual tension.... It may be supposed that, as a result of an appropriate stimulation of

Conclusion

Darwin, Haeckel, and Fliess broadened the scope of sexuality beyond genitality. Considering thumb-sucking or any other infantile pleasure as a sexual activity is not the "privilege" of psychoanalysis. It cannot even be decided by psychoanalysis. In *Instincts and Their Vicissitudes* (1915), Freud will be very explicit about it: "I am altogether doubtful whether any decisive pointers for the differentiation and classification of the instincts can be arrived at on the basis of working over the psychological material." (Freud 1915, 124) According to Freud, the sexual character of infantile sexuality can only be determined by evolutionary biology and endocrinology.[21]

erotogenic zones, or in other circumstances that are accompanied by an onset of sexual excitation, some substance that is disseminated generally throughout the organism becomes decomposed and the products of its decomposition give rise to a specific stimulus which acts on the reproductive organs or upon a spinal centre related to them." (Freud 1905, 215)

[21] "Biology teaches that sexuality is not to be put on a par with other functions of the individual.... The hypothesis that the sexual function differs from other bodily processes in virtue of a special chemistry is, I understand, also a postulate of the Ehrlich school of biological research." (Freud 1915, 125)

3. The Constitution of Sexual Phantasy

Between 1908 and 1915, Freud tried to understand the *sexual phantasies of children* and the *perverse relation*. In 1908, he published *On the Sexual Theories of Children* and, in 1909, the case-study of the first psychoanalysis of a child, *Analysis of a Phobia in a Five-Year-Old Boy* [Little Hans]. In these works, he develops a theory about the sexual phantasies of children. According to Freud, these phantasies must be analysed as infantile theories about adult sexuality. Children do not understand the sexuality of their parents and they invent theories to understand adult sexuality. However, these theories can never attain the truth because the child does not know the female genitals.[1] He thinks that everyone has a penis. Therefore, all these theories will be *monosexual* theories about adult sexuality. According to Freud, this monosexuality of infantile sexology plays an important role in our sexual object-choice as adults. In his study of Leonardo da Vinci, *Leonardo da Vinci and a Memory of his Childhood* (1910), Freud shows how Leonardo's homosexuality is related to these infantile sexual theories. In *On the Universal Tendency to Debasement in the Sphere of Love* (1912), he analyses the infantile phantasy in the sexual object choice of neurotics, and in *Instincts and their Vicissitudes* (1915), he analyses the perverse relation.

The Sexual Phantasies of Children

In his scientific notebooks, Leonardo writes that when he was a little child in the cradle, "a vulture came down to me, and opened my mouth with its tail, and struck me many times with its tail against my lips." (Freud 1910, 82) But, according to Freud, it is impossible that Leonardo could have retained such an early memory. It is not a memory but a phantasy, which is produced later and projected back into childhood. However, this does not mean that nothing happened in childhood or that the phantasy is completely devoid of historical truth. Here Freud repeats a point of view which he already expressed in a letter to Fliess of 3 January 1899: "Phantasies are products of later periods and are projected back from what was then the present into earliest childhood.... To the question 'What happened in earliest childhood?' the answer is, 'Nothing, but the germ of a sexual impulse existed'." (Freud 1985, 338) Leonardo's phantasy about the vulture that opened his mouth can be traced back to "nothing but the germ of a sexual impulse". According to Freud, "What the phantasy conceals is merely a reminiscence of sucking—or being suckled—at his mother's breast." (Freud 1910, 87)

---

[1] It is obvious that in this case Freud only speaks about the boy.

Up until now, Freud's interpretation of Leonardo's early childhood is in accordance with what he said in the *Three Essays* (1905). In 1905, Freud maintained that infantile sexuality was an organic process, which was not yet supported by phantasies. In a case-study published in the same year as the *Three Essays* (1905),[2] Freud says that his patient's sexual phantasy of *fellatio* is produced in puberty. Only the preference for an *oral* sexual phantasy is determined by the fact that, as a child, the patient, Dora, had been an ardent thumb-sucker. (Freud 1905, 51) In 1910, Freud states this view even more clearly: "The *organic impression* of this experience [sucking the mother's breast]—the first source of pleasure in our life—doubtless remains indelibly *printed* on us; and when at *a later date* the child becomes familiar with the cow's udder whose function is that of a nipple, but whose shape and position under the belly make it resemble a penis, the preliminary stage has been reached which will *later* enable him to form the repellent sexual phantasy." (Freud 1910, 87, my emphasis) Sexual phantasies are produced later, and are supported by an infantile factor, which is merely an organic impression printed on us.

But why the vulture in Leonardo's phantasy? According to Freud, Leonardo must have known the ancient idea that there are only female vultures. He must also have been familiar with the theory about how they are impregnated: "At a certain time these birds pause in mid-flight, open their vagina and are impregnated by the wind." (Freud 1910, 89) The Fathers of the Church used this theory as an argument for the Virgin Birth. When Leonardo read about this theory, it awoke a memory in him. During the first years of his life, he had had a mother but no father; only later would he be "adopted" by his father and his stepmother. According to Freud, the fact that the (all female) vultures remind him of his early years alone with his mother implies that the young Leonardo must have been aware of his father's absence at the time. (Freud 1910, 91) Freud needs this awareness to understand Leonardo's famous thirst for knowledge. According to Freud, because of the awareness of his father's absence, Leonardo began to "brood on this riddle with special intensity, and so at a tender age became a researcher, tormented as he was by the great question of where babies come from and what the father has to do with their origin." (Freud 1910, 92)

In the analysis of Little Hans,[3] Freud discovered the sexual theories of childhood, which discovery was a completely new addition to Freud's sexual theory. The chapter on "Infantile Sexology" in the *Three Essays* was only added in 1915. In *On the Sexual Theories of Children* (1908), Freud describes how children are confronted with three problems concerning the sexuality of adults: What is the difference between men and women? Where do babies come from? And what is the meaning of sexual intercourse? In this paper, Freud presents the desperate struggle of children to answer these riddles.

---

[2] *Fragment of an Analysis of a Case of Hysteria* (1905).
[3] *Analysis of a Phobia in a Five-Year-Old Boy* (1909).

Where do babies come from? This is "the first, grand problem of life." (Freud 1908, 212) According to Freud, this is not a purely intellectual question for the child. Thinking is not born out of curiosity, but out of despair: "A child's desire for knowledge on this point does not in fact awaken spontaneously, prompted perhaps by some inborn need for established causes; it is aroused under the goad of the self-seeking (*eigensüchtigen*) instincts that dominate him, when—perhaps after the end of his second year—he is confronted with the arrival of a new baby." (Freud 1908, 212) The child's primary reaction to this new baby is one of hostility, because he experiences a loss of love and care from his parents, whose attention is centred for the moment on the newcomer.[4] This traumatic intrusion of the new baby awakens the child's desire for knowledge. He needs this knowledge to prevent such terrible things from happening in the future.[5]

Confronted with this first enigma, the child turns to his parents for an answer. But this appeal to the adults only reveals their dishonesty. The evasive answers of the parents ("The stork brings the babies", etc.) do not convince the child. This does not mean, however, that the answers of the adults remain without effect. They produce a distrust of adults. From now on, the child is alone in his search for the truth.[6] This double disillusionment (the arrival of the new baby and the dishonesty of the adults) produces a first psychical conflict. (1908, 214) On the one hand, the child remains a "good boy" who adheres to the explanations given him by his parents. He becomes obedient and, consequently, stupid.[7] On the other hand, the child nurtures his hostility of the new rival and his need to understand in secret. The conflict between these two trends, says Freud, leads to a dissociation (*Spaltung*) of the psyche. (1908, 214) This dissociation constitutes the "nuclear complex of a neurosis". According to Jean Laplanche, Freud's reference to this dissociation must be considered as an hypothesis about the origin of the unconscious (Laplanche 1980b, 34). In any case, the lies of the adults produce the possibility of secret research.

[4] "During the first few days he was naturally put very much in the background. He was suddenly taken ill with a sore throat. In the fever he was heard saying: 'But I don't *want* a baby sister'." (Freud 1909, 11)

[5] "The question itself is, like all research, the product of a *vital* exigency, as though thinking were entrusted with the task of preventing the recurrence of such dreaded events." (Freud 1908, 213, my emphasis)

[6] "It seems to me to follow from a great deal of information I have received that children refuse to believe the stork theory and that from the time of this first deception and rebuff they nourish a distrust of adults and have a suspicion of there being something forbidden which is being withheld from them by the 'grown-ups', and that they consequently hide their further researches under the cloak of secrecy." (1908, 213)

[7] "The set of views which are bound up with being 'good', but also with *a cessation of reflection*, become the dominant and conscious one." (1908, 214, my emphasis)

The boy cannot understand where babies come from because he takes it for granted that everyone, male or female, has a "widdler". Babies grow inside the mother. But how did they get there and how do they get out? The child's ignorance of the vagina and of the role of the father in conception leads him to false theories that are based on the experience of his own body: "If the baby grows in the mother's body and is removed from it, this can only happen along the one possible pathway—the anal aperture. *The baby must be evacuated like a piece of excrement, like a stool.*" (Freud 1908, 219) The child also uses the experience of his own body to answer the question how the baby gets inside the mother: "One eats some particular thing and gets a child from it." (1908, 220) Eating and defecating are the only possible answers to the child because he does not know the female genitals.

According to Freud, there are three typical childhood phantasies.[8] The first is the idea that all human beings have a penis. The second theory consists of a conception of birth as an oral or anal event. The third theory is the sadistic interpretation of sexual intercourse. It is clear from what we have said before that the first two of these theories are closely connected. It is because the boy believes that everyone is like himself, that he cannot solve the problem of conception and birth. The problem of sexual intercourse, on the other hand, has no connection with the problem of birth: "It appears more often that the connection is overlooked by them for the very reason that they have interpreted the act of love as an act of violence." (Freud 1908, 221) When they witness or overhear the sexual intercourse between their parents, they interpret it sadistically, informed in this by the sadistic impulses of their own infantile sexuality. In general, their interpretations depend upon the state of their own sexuality.[9] This becomes manifest in the answers children give to the question what it means to be married: "The notion I have most frequently met with is that *each of the married couple urinates in front of the other.*" (1908, 222)

Infantile sexual theories are informed by infantile sexuality. Still, infantile sexology and infantile sexuality must be clearly distinguished from each other. Infantile sexuality consists of partial impulses, which originate in an erotogenic zone that is not necessarily genital. The infantile sexual theories on the other hand are answers to the enigmas of *adult* sexuality. According to Freud, the child has no knowledge of the vagina and of the role of the father. (1908, 218) The riddles of adult sexuality therefore cannot be solved, and the child will fill the gaps in his knowledge in accordance with his own infantile sexuality. In this way, the organic processes of infantile sexuality begin to play a

---

[8] When Freud speaks about childhood phantasies, he only refers to the boy.
[9] "He answers the question differently according as his chance perceptions in relation to his parents have coincided with instincts of his own which are still pleasurably coloured." (1908, 222)

part in the child's phantasy-life.[10] Infantile sexology is thus not a part of infantile sexuality as such, but the result of a confrontation between infantile and adult sexuality. The oral theory of conception, for instance, is an answer to an enigma of adult sexuality, but it is an answer that is informed by the child's own pleasure in thumb-sucking. Only now becomes the oral erotogenic zone invested with phantasies. The pleasurable experiences of infancy support the child's "perverse" answers to the troubling enigmas of adult sexuality, and sexual phantasies are therefore essentially "confusions" between infantile and adult sexuality. This shows that there is a complex connection between autoerotism and sexual phantasy. Sexual phantasy is not just the mental counterpart of autoerotism.[11]

The discovery of infantile sexology leads Freud to a "phallocentric" conception of sexual phantasies. The first sexual theory of children consists in the idea that every human being has a penis. This idea then becomes the cornerstone of all the sexual phantasies of children, for it is because of this idea that they are unable to solve the problem of birth, conception, and sexual intercourse.

In *The Sexual Theories of Children* (1908), Freud describes these infantile sexual theories, but he does not say much about how the child ever gets out of his monosexual universe. He seems to assume that most children grow out of it when they start to learn from experience and from each other. There are some people, however, who remain fixated to this monosexual phase. According to Freud, those children who will later become homosexuals have been terrorised by a threat of castration. Because of this threat they will interpret the vagina as a mutilated organ, and it is only when this happens that the vagina provokes horror in them instead of pleasure, leading to homosexuality in later life.[12] Although Freud introduces the castration-complex in 1908, it does not yet have the universality it will have in his later thought. In 1908, the castration-complex is not regarded by Freud as an essential element in the constitution of the subject, but as a traumatic experience restricted to the aetiology of homosexuality (Laplanche 1980b, 41). In most cases, the infantile research is broken off, not by the threat of castration, but "in helpless perplexity." (Freud 1908, 218)[13]

---

[10] "After so many détours an organic correspondence reappears in the psychical sphere as an unconscious identity." (Freud 1917, 133)

[11] Therefore, Freud's theory about the constitution of phantasy is a much more complicated theory that the Kleinian idea about phantasy. See S. Isaacs (1991)

[12] "The woman's genitalia, when seen later on, are regarded as a mutilated organ and recall this threat, and they therefore arouse horror instead of pleasure in the homosexual." (Freud 1908, 217)

[13] Castration is a crucial element in the analysis of Little Hans. This analysis shows, however, that the threat of castration itself has no power to produce a terrorising effect. Freud emphasises that the boy is not impressed at all when his mother threatens him that the doctor will come and cut off his penis: "She threatens him in these words: 'If you do that [touch his penis], I shall send for Dr. A. to cut off your widdler. And then what'll you widdle with?' *Hans*: 'With my bottom'. He

The introduction of infantile sex*ology* is a crucial step in Freud's thinking. In 1905, Freud considered infantile sexuality as purely autoerotic. In 1908, however, he describes how the enigmas of adult sexuality initiate the constitution of sexual phantasies in childhood. This does not mean that he gives up his idea about autoerotism. Freud holds on to his idea that infantile sexuality as such is an organic process. But now Freud understands that *already in childhood* these organic processes of the child's own sexuality provide non-genital answers to the enigmas of adult sexuality. The child is unable to understand the sexuality of adults because he lives in a monosexual, phallic world.[14] This monosexuality of infantile sexology will have a decisive influence on the child's later sexual object-choice because, in childhood and in the unconscious, there is no genital sexuality. We will show how these infantile phantasies determine object-choice in neurosis, homosexuality and perversion.

Monosexuality and Object-Choice

In *On Narcissism: An Introduction* (1914), Freud distinguishes two types of sexual object-choice: the anaclitic and the narcissistic. The anaclitic object-choice is modelled on the relation with the mother and on the sexual satisfactions experienced in the early relation with her. (1914, 87) But this is only one

---

made this reply without having any sense of guilt as yet." (1909, 8) The threat has no effect on his sexual curiosity. Even after the threat he produces typical sexual theories of anal birth and he keeps on thinking that everyone has a "widdler". It is only much later that he will show a deferred obedience to the threat of castration. But, what happened in the meantime to produce this *nachträglich* traumatic effect of the threat? "The great event of Hans's life," says Freud, is the birth of his sister Hannah. (1909, 10) The beginning of his interest in "widdlers" coincides with the second trimester of his mother's pregnancy. When Hannah is born, Hans reacts with hostility and jealousy. After a few days, however, his envy is overcome because of his focus on the problem of "widdlers": "A little later Hans was watching his seven-day-old sister being given a bath. 'But her widdler's still quite small,' he remarked." (1909, 11) In this way, Hans establishes a connection between his hostility and the question of big and small "widdlers". Because of this connection, his later friendliness towards his sister will always be accompanied by a feeling of superiority. (1909, 11) Once the problem of jealousy is decided on the level of "widdlers", Hans is introduced into a hostility towards his father, which occupies the whole of the analysis. In the case history of little Hans, however, Freud seems to neglect what he had emphasised in *On the Sexual Theories of Children*: that the desire for knowledge about sexual matters results from a *vital* threat, i.e. the arrival of a new baby. It is only when it becomes associated with this vital threat that the threat of castration becomes effective. This idea of castration as a symbolisation of a more primordial mortification will remain in the background of Freud's thinking.

[14] We will come back to the relation between autoerotism and infantile phantasies later in this chapter.

type of object-choice: "We have discovered, especially clearly in people whose libidinal development has suffered some disturbance, such as perverts and homosexuals, that in their later choice of love-objects they have taken as a model not their mother but their own selves." (1914, 88) The narcissistic type of object-choice is typical for perverts and homosexuals. This does not mean, of course, that the anaclitic type is normal. For Freud, the opposite of perversion is not normality, but neurosis. The anaclitic object-choice too is motivated by the monosexual phantasies of childhood. First, we will show why the anaclitic object-choice belongs to the domain of neurosis, and then we will discuss the narcissistic object-choice in homosexuality and perversion.

In the third essay of the *Three Essays* (1905), "The Transformations of Puberty", Freud describes the different phases in the finding of a sexual object. The finding of a sexual object after puberty is, according to Freud, a refinding of it. (1905, 222) The first object of the infant's sexual instinct is the breast. It is only when the breast is given up that the sexual instinct becomes autoerotic, in thumb-sucking. At puberty, organic processes instigate sexual differentiation and the search for a sexual object. At first, object-choice is only performed in phantasy, and "in these phantasies the infantile tendencies invariably emerge once more, but this time with intensified pressure from somatic sources." (1905, 226-7) These phantasies involve the same persons as the ones the libido was originally attached to in childhood, but because of their incestuous nature, these phantasies are repudiated: "By the postponing of sexual maturation, time has been gained in which the child can erect, among other restraints on sexuality, the barrier against incest.... Respect for this barrier is essentially a cultural demand made by society." (1905, 225) In severe psychoneuroses, the incestuous phantasies produce a total inhibition of adult sexuality and a life-long devotion to the parents.[15] But the psychoneuroses, says Freud, only show in an exaggerated form the universal misery of love.

In *On the Universal Tendency to Debasement in the Sphere of Love* (1912), Freud describes and analyses this misery in further detail. In this text, Freud goes on to analyse the relation between object-choice, sexuality, and the incest taboo. In the first part of this paper, he discusses the clinical problem of psychic impotence. This impotence, says Freud, is the symptom of a fixation to incestuous phantasies.[16] In most cases, however, this does not lead to total

---

[15] Freud insists on the sexual nature of this love: "They are mostly girls, who, to the delight of their parents, have persisted in all their childish love far beyond puberty. It is most instructive to find that it is precisely these girls who in their later marriage lack the capacity to give their husbands what is due to them; they make cold wives and remain sexually anaesthetic. We learn from this that sexual love and what appears to be non-sexual love for parents are fed from the same sources." (1905, 227)

[16] "In this way it can happen that the whole of a young man's sensuality becomes tied to incestuous objects in the unconscious, or to put it another way, becomes fixated to unconscious incestuous phantasies. The result is total impotence." (1912, 182)

impotence, but to a lack of pleasure in sexual intercourse with the person they love and respect. (1912, 183) But if these same men have sex with a prostitute, they experience a peculiar increase of their sexual pleasure: "As soon as the condition of debasement is fulfilled, sensuality can be freely expressed, and important sexual capacities and a high degree of pleasure can develop." (1912, 183) These men show an idealisation of the woman who is a mother-substitute, while they can only obtain sexual pleasure with a woman who does not remind them of their mothers or sisters. According to Freud, this clinical picture is not restricted to pathology: "This behaviour does in fact characterise the love of civilized man." (1912, 184) The conflict between love and sexual pleasure is insurmountable because of the incest taboo.[17]

In the third part of his paper,[18] Freud gives a deeper analysis of this conflict between love and sexual pleasure. In the end, our misery cannot be blamed on society and the incest taboo it imposes: "Something in the nature of the sexual instinct itself is unfavourable to the realization of complete satisfaction." (1912, 188) At the time of puberty, the component instincts must be united under the primacy of the genitals.[19] But this unification always fails partially. This failure is due, not to the pressure of society, but to *organic* repression.[20] The infantile pleasures that cannot be integrated into adult, genital sexuality "can be detected in sexual activity in the form of *non-satisfaction*." (1912, 190, my emphasis) So, it is not just the incestuous nature of our phantasies that prevents total satisfaction. The organic repression of infantile, especially anal, pleasures produces afterwards disgust and shame, or at least non-satisfaction. In this way, Freud traced the conflict between love and sexuality back to "universal characteristics of our organic instincts." (1912, 188) In and beyond adult, genital, sexuality, the neurotic is confronted with the *repression* of his infantile relation to the mother and of his autoerotic pleasures. He reacts with disgust, shame and non-satisfaction.

The narcissistic object-choice of homosexuals and perverts, it seems, is a solution to this misery. In his study on Leonardo, Freud analyses Leonardo's (ideal) homosexuality. According to Freud, Leonardo's vulture phantasy must

[17] "Anyone who is to be really free and happy in love must have surmounted his respect for women and have come to terms with the idea of incest with his mother or sister." (1912, 186)
[18] *On the Universal Tendency to Debasement in the Sphere of Love* (1912).
[19] "The final outcome of sexual development lies in what is known as the normal sexual life of the adult, in which the pursuit of pleasure comes under the sway of the reproductive function and in which the component instincts, under the primacy of a single erotogenic zone, form a firm organization directed towards a sexual aim attached to some extraneous sexual object." (1905, 197)
[20] "These above all the coprophilic instinctual components, which have proved incompatible with our aesthetic standards of culture, probably since, as a result of our adopting an erect gait, we raised our organ of smell from the ground. The same is true of a large portion of the sadistic urges which are part of erotic life." (1912, 189)

be traced back to the experience of sucking the mother's breast. In the vulture phantasy, however, it has become a phantasy that symbolises an act of fellatio: "It resembles certain dreams and phantasies found in women and passive homosexuals." (1910, 86) This implies, for Freud, that the vulture with its tail represents the typical phantasy of a woman with a penis.[21]

In the *Three Essays*, Freud had already remarked that homosexuals do not just look for a male sexual object, but for an object with female features and a male sexual organ: "The sexual object is not someone of the same sex but someone who combines the characters of both sexes; there is, as it were, a compromise between an impulse that seeks for a man and one that seeks for a woman, while it remains a paramount condition that the sexual object's body (i.e. genitals) shall be masculine." (1905, 144) The homosexual object-choice thus reveals the fixation to the monosexual phase, when the child assumed that everyone has a penis.[22] This fixation originates at the time of an early, intense erotic attachment to the mother. In the case of Leonardo, this erotic bond between mother and child was intensified by the fact that in his earliest years, Leonardo lived alone with his mother because his father was absent. (1910, 99) Later, this close relation to the mother is repressed.[23]

During puberty, however, the homosexual finds a way to return to this lost state of bliss. "The boy represses his love for his mother: he puts himself in her place, identifies himself with her, and takes his own person as a model in whose likeness he chooses the new objects of his love. In this way he has become homosexual. What he has in fact done is to slip back to autoerotism." (1910, 100) According to Freud, this is the trajectory that constitutes a *narcissistic* object-choice. The other is just another me and I identify myself with my mother.[24] This identification is supported by the monosexuality of childhood:

---

21 "The vulture-headed Egyptian goddess Mutt... was usually represented by the Egyptians with a phallus; her body was female, as the breasts indicated, but it also had a male organ in a state of erection." (1910, 94)

22 This does not mean that the anaclitic lover does not have this fixation to the monosexual phase. He, too, is not looking for a sexual partner of the opposite sex. He is in search of a mother. In homosexuality, however, the monosexuality of *every* child reveals itself in a clearer way. See *Three Essays*: "Psychoanalysis considers that a choice of an object *independently of its sex*—freedom to range equally over male and female objects—as it is found in childhood, in primitive states of society and early periods of history, is the original basis from which, as a result of restriction in one direction or the other, both the normal and the inverted types develop." (1905, 145, my emphasis)

23 Freud does not mention what motivates this repression. Is the bond with the mother abandoned because of a threat of castration, or because of organic repression? Freud does not answer the question how this blissful union is lost. In the case of Leonardo, this does not present a problem because at the age of five Leonardo is taken away from his mother to live with his father and stepmother. In 1910, Freud only says that the close bond with the mother is lost in one way or another.

24 "They look for a young man who resembles themselves and whom *they* may love as their mother loved *them*." (1905, 145, 56)

Like me, my mother has a penis.²⁵ In his Schreber case study, Freud gives a clearer analysis of the narcissistic object-choice. He emphasises how a narcissistic object-choice is constituted in two phases. First, there is a transition from autoerotism to self-love: 'My mother loves me' is transformed into 'I love myself as my mother loved me.' In a second phase, self-love is transformed in love of another: 'I love you as I love myself as my mother loved me.'

The Narcissistic Object-choice of Perverts

In the *Three Essays* (1905), Freud was unable to explain sadomasochism and voyeurism-exhibitionism because he did not understand the perverse *relation*²⁶ and because he could not find the *autoerotic* pleasure underlying these perversions.²⁷ These two problems, it will appear, are intimately connected. Freud could not trace back sadomasochism and scopophilia to autoerotism. In *Instincts and their Vicissitudes* (1915), it becomes clear why. Thumb-sucking, for instance, is objectless, because its "object" coincides with its source (the lips).²⁸ In *Instincts and their Vicissitudes*, Freud admits that this concept of autoerotism cannot account for sadomasochism and voyeurism-exhibitionism: "The object of the scopophilic instinct, however, though it too is in the first instance a part of the subject's own body, is *not the eye itself*; and in sadism the organic source, which is probably the muscular apparatus with its capacity for action, points unequivocally at *an object other than itself*, even though that object is part of the subject's own body." (1915, 132, my emphasis) Because of this split between the source and the object, sadism and voyeurism differ from autoerotism.

Here Freud overcomes his failure in the *Three Essays* to find the infantile autoerotic source of sadism and masochism. In 1915, he acknowledges that it is impossible to trace sadism and voyeurism back to a purely autoerotic pleasure, because in the infantile activities underlying these perversions there is always already a split between their source and their object. Because of this split between source and object, Freud cannot rely on his earlier concept of

---

[25] "People who are manifest homosexuals in later life have, it may be presumed, never emancipated themselves from the binding condition that the object of their choice must possess genitals like their own; and in this connection the infantile sexual theories which attribute the same kind of genitals to both sexes exert much influence." (1911, 61)

[26] I.e. why "a sadist is always at the same time a masochist." (1905, 159)

[27] Freud, 1905, 158

[28] The thumb is not the "object" of thumb-sucking. It is only an aid in the play of pure auto-affection: "The inferiority of this second zone is among the reasons why at a later date he seeks the corresponding part—the lips—of another person. ('It's a pity I can't kiss myself', he seems to be saying.)" (1905, 182)

autoerotism anymore. Therefore, it seems, he introduces the concept of narcissism as a substitute for "autoerotism".[29]

The step from autoerotism to narcissism, however, implies a radically different interpretation of the first phase of sexual life. While autoerotism involved the idea of a pure affectation of self by self, narcissism implies the difference between a subject and an object, which in narcissism are united in the same individual. With the introduction of narcissism, "auto-affection" (the self-self of the lips) is replaced by "reflexivity" (subject-object).[30] This distinction between a subject and an object is anticipated by the split between source and object. Hurting yourself or looking at yourself is reflexive in a way thumb-sucking is not—thumb-sucking is not "sucking yourself".

This difference between autoerotic and reflexive activities reflects the difference between the two types of object-choice: the anaclitic and the narcissistic. The anaclitic object-choice is modelled on the relation with the mother and on the sexual satisfactions experienced in the early relation with her. (1914, 87) In the preceding paragraphs, we have described this type of object-choice and the misery it involves. The introduction of a narcissistic type of object-choice, however, opens up the possibility of understanding the perverse relation as a "solution" to the misery of love. Narcissistic object-choice defends the subject against the troubles connected with the incest-taboo. His love-object does not remind him of his mother or his sister, but of himself.

As we have seen, however, the misery of the anaclitic lover cannot be blamed on the incest-taboo alone. Total satisfaction is made impossible first of all by the organic repression of infantile sexuality (i.e. the abandonment of erotogenic zones). This leads in adult sexuality to a partial non-satisfaction. In the perverse relation, however, the barriers of disgust, shame, and non-satisfaction seem to have been overcome.[31] But the price to be paid for this is the *reflexivity* of the subject's sexual activities. What does this mean?

Freud seems to understand this reflexivity on two different levels. First, there is a reflexivity between subject and object. The other of the perverse relation is only another "me".[32] Exhibitionism and voyeurism are transformations of an

---

[29] "We have become accustomed to call the early phase of the development of the ego, during which its sexual instincts find autoerotic satisfaction, 'narcissism', without at once entering on any discussion of the relation between autoerotism and narcissism. It follows that the preliminary stage of the scopophilic instinct, in which the subject's own body is the object of the scopophilia, must be classed under narcissism, and that we must describe it as a narcissistic formation." (1915, 131-2)

[30] Freud himself refers to this reflexivity, without clearly distinguishing it from auto-affection. (1915, 128)

[31] See, for instance, Birch (1999).

[32] "An extraneous person is once more sought as object; this person, in consequence of the alteration which has taken place in the instinctual aim, has to take over the role of the subject..... Here, too, satisfaction follows along the path of the original sadism, the passive ego placing itself back in phantasy in its first role, which has now in fact been taken over by the extraneous subject." (1915, 128)

earlier phase in which the subject looks at himself. In the manifest perversions, the active or the passive role is taken over by another. But this reflexivity between subject and object was already foreshadowed by the split between the source and the object, between the eye and what is looked at, or between the power of the muscles and what they overpower. When I look at myself, my eye does not look at itself, but at another part of my body. This split introduces a distance which becomes manifest in the perverse relation.

In the phenomenology of perversion, therefore, one notices a heightening of self-awareness. There is no kissing and no self-forgetfulness. The enactment of the perverse scenario presupposes a continual distance between the eye and the other erotogenic zones.[33] If the perverse relation appears to refind the lost pleasures of childhood, to slip back into autoerotism, it is only "in play" (1924, 162), "at a distance" (1905, 204). One of Mc Dougall's patients tells her that for him life is just a game. In the analysis, he becomes aware of the fact that this "game" is supported by an anonymous gaze. In his work and in the sadism that constitutes his sex-life, he has the feeling of performing in front of an audience. As long as he "acts" for an audience, he is capable of anything (McDougall 1980).

Narcissism, therefore, is not identical with autoerotism. Narcissism is an *image* of autoerotism, translated on the level of object-love, and thus *enacting* the blissful union of childhood. In this way, the pleasure of childhood has been transformed into an *image* of childhood happiness. In *On Narcissism: An Introduction*, Freud describes this crucial difference between autoerotism and narcissism as follows: "The return of the object-love to the ego and its transformation into narcissism *represents* [*Darstellt*], as it were, a happy love once more; and, *on the other hand*, it is true that a real happy love corresponds to the primal condition in which object-libido and ego-libido cannot be distinguished." (1914, 100, my emphasis) Narcissism is essentially on the level of an image, a *Darstellung*.

This interpretation of narcissism as *an image of* autoerotism can elucidate Freud's analysis of sadomasochism in *Instincts and their Vicissitudes* (1915). According to Freud, the genesis of sadomasochism must be described as a development in two steps. In a first phase, there is the will to overpower the object. When Freud says that this is already sadism, then this 'sadism' must be understood in a very broad sense of aggressiveness towards the object. In the second phase, "the object is given up and replaced by the subject's self." (1915, 127) Freud describes this phase with an allusion to the voices of the Greek verb: "The active voice is changed, not into the passive, but into the reflexive, middle voice." (1915, 128)

---

[33] For a clinical elaboration, see: McDougall 1980. In *Bad Penny*, Penny tells how she was introduced in the pleasures of being beaten. While she was being beaten by her aunt, she was not excited by the feelings of pain itself, but by watching the beating in a mirror. (Burch 1999, 21)

When Freud says that "the object is given up", this means that the real object is given up and that an image of the object is installed in the subject. In this way, there is not only a transition from activity to reflexivity, but also one from external reality to phantasy. (Laplanche 1980a, 293) The aggressive scene is transformed into a sadomasochistic scenario. Masochism proper (the third phase) is only possible when it is supported by this sadomasochistic phantasy. In masochism, the subject takes the passive role and identifies with a sadistic role played by another person. This identification is possible because the sadist is only an actor in *my* masochistic scenario. We could say that he is just 'another me.' From this analysis of sadomasochism, it is clear that according to Freud, perversion implies a narcissistic object-choice. Perverse pleasure is conditioned by the enactment of a scenario; perversion is performance, *Darstellung*.

In *The Many Faces of Eros*, Mc Dougall presents a case that reveals this reflexivity in a remarkable way. A woman comes into analysis complaining of phobias. In the course of her analysis, she tells the analyst that her husband can only be sexually excited when she urinates on him. Although this disgusts her, she complies with his wishes. Later in the analysis, however, she remembers a peculiar scene from her childhood. When she was three or four years old, three boys persuaded her to take off her pants and climb a tree so that they could see her sex. Once she was up the tree they demanded that she urinate. She started to do so and it gave her a feeling of pleasure and triumph, but then she was caught in the act by her nanny, who gave her a thrashing. (McDougall 1995)

This memory reveals how the patient's husband apparently plays a part in her unconscious sexual scenario. The case is thus a surprising illustration of the fact that the other is only another me, an actor in my phantasy. In this example, the woman plays the same role as in the scene of her childhood. But the point is that every phantasy contains a scenario for *two* actors. This shows why Freud had to introduce narcissism to explain the fact that "a sadist is always at the same time a masochist" (1905, 159)[34] Every sadist is always also a masochist, and vice versa, because their pleasure depends on the sadomasochistic *phantasy* rather than on their *position* in the phantasy.

This analysis of sadomasochism explains the mystery that there can be pleasure in pain. Pain as such cannot be a source of pleasure. It is a sadistic pleasure turned upon one's own self. Pleasure in pain, therefore, depends entirely upon the phantasy and upon the identification of the masochist with the sadist.

However, Freud's analysis of sadomasochism is not as unproblematic as we have presented it so far. In his description of the genesis of sadomasochism,

---

[34] In *Instincts and their Vicissitudes* (1915), Freud says, "The instinctual vicissitudes which consist in the instinct's being turned round upon the subject's own ego and undergoing reversal from activity to passivity are dependent on the narcissistic organization of the ego and bear the stamp of that phase." (1915, 132)

there are two kinds of sadism. On the one hand, there is the sadism of the first phase. Freud describes this sadism as "the exercise of violence or power upon some other person as object." (1915, 127) It is not clear from this description what is sexual or perverse about it. It is aggression, but not sexual aggression. Freud seems to be aware of this when he stresses that this "sadism" is not interested in inflicting pain: "A sadistic child takes no account of whether or not he inflicts pains, nor does he intend to do so." (1915, 128) Freud's primary sadism is not a sexual perversion; it refers rather to an originary, pre-sexual *ruthlessness*.

On the other hand, however, there is the sadism of the third phase. In this phase, sadism is the active pole of the sadomasochistic phantasy. This is definitely a sexual perversion. This is the sadist who wants to inflict pain and who enjoys doing so. But even this sadism does not seem to fit the descriptions of sex-murderers in Krafft-Ebing. Freud's sadist is only an actor in the sadomasochistic game. His role always remains supported and limited by the masochist's phantasy. Freud's analysis of sadism fits Wanda von Dunajew, the accomplice of Sacher Masoch. In *The Economic Problem of Masochism* (1924), Freud will implicitly mention this difference between "real" sadism and the sadist of the sadomasochistic phantasy when he says that "masochistic tortures, incidentally, rarely make such a serious impression as the cruelties of sadism, whether imagined or performed." (1924, 162)

Conclusion

In the analyses of little Hans and of Leonardo, Freud discovers the way in which sexual phantasies are constituted. Confronted with the enigmas of adult sexuality, the child creates sexual theories in accordance with its own infantile sexuality. These theories are all characterised by the presupposition that all human beings have a penis. These monosexual phantasies are the condition for sexual object-choice. This is most clear in the object-choice of homosexuals, which is based on an identification with the mother of the monosexual phase.

This analysis of childhood phantasies shows that infantile sexuality is not limited to autoerotism. The child has sexual phantasies, but they are not genital phantasies. Because the child does not know the female genitals or the function of the father in procreation, he develops theories which are necessarily "perverse" because they are informed by the child's own non-genital pleasures. This is an important addition to the sexual theory of the first edition of *Three Essays* (1905) in which infantile sexuality was considered as autoerotic and objectless. In 1905, Freud held the view that sexual phantasies were constituted in puberty. (Freud 1905, 226) The analysis of little Hans changed his mind about this. Of course, the child's own sexuality remains autoerotic and objectless, but the child also produces theories about adult sexuality. These phantasies are informed by his own pleasures.

Before 1915, Freud was unable to understand the reflexivity of perverse relations. But in *Instincts and their Vicissitudes* (1915), he discovers the infantile factor in sadomasochism and in scopophilia. Looking at yourself and hurting yourself are not autoerotic, but reflexive activities. The eye does not look at itself, but at another part of the body. In this way, the muscles (sadism) and the gaze (voyeurism) anticipate an object. They push the sexual instinct out of its autoerotism towards an outer object. At the same time, however, this object remains just another me, because the relation to this object remains the heir of the narcissistic stage in which I look at *myself* and in which I master *myself*.

In the next chapter, we will see how these reflexive, monosexual phantasies are destroyed in psychosis, in such a way that the other cannot appear as another me anymore. This will also highlight the anthropological dimension of Freud's analysis of perverse phantasies. According to Freud, these perverse phantasies are the prototypes for the object-relations of all human beings.

4. The Destruction of Sexual Phantasy

In 1906, C.G. Jung starts his correspondence with Freud.[1] Unlike Freud, Jung is a psychiatrist who works mainly with schizophrenic patients. He has become interested in psychoanalysis because he believes that Freud's insights might be helpful in the psychology and psychotherapy of psychosis, and in the course of their correspondence, Freud too becomes interested in the problem of psychosis.

At first, Freud tries to apply his theory of the neuroses to psychosis (schizophrenia and paranoia) as well. This is the aim of his study of Schreber, *Psychoanalytic Notes on an Autobiographical Account of a Case of Paranoia (Dementia Paranoides)* (1911). In the course of the collaboration between Freud and Jung, however, it becomes clear to both of them that their theories of psychosis differ radically. According to Jung, psychosis is characterised by a withdrawal into a phantasy-world. For Freud, psychosis has to do with the destruction of sexual phantasy. Since our capacity to relate to an object depends on these phantasies[2] (see previous chapter), the destruction of phantasy, at the same time, abolishes our object-relations.

The Initial Misunderstanding

In April 1907, Freud sends a letter to Jung, which is entitled "A Few Remarks on Paranoia". In this letter (22F)[3] and in the next one (23F), Freud sketches his thoughts about the psychological mechanisms underlying paranoia and schizophrenia. According to Freud, the "perception" of being persecuted by an object is a consequence of the withdrawal of libido from the image of the object. This leaves the libido without an object. Not only is the real object lost; so, too, is the *image* of the object, and the libido thereby becomes objectless and therefore autoerotic. This is what happens in schizophrenia. The delusions of persecution that are typical of paranoia are attempts to re-cathect the object: "The libido returns to its object, tries to prevail, and with a reversal to unpleasure clings to the perceptions into which the object has been transformed" (22F).[4] In paranoia, then, there is an intense relation to an object again, but this

---

[1] For a detailed historical and theoretical study of the encounter between Freud and Jung, see Vandermeersch (1991).
[2] In Freud's theory, only the reflexive phantasy in which the other is another me, can explain our sexual interest in objects. Without these phantasies the sexual instincts would remain in a state of autoerotic pleasure.
[3] McGuire (1974).
[4] We will elucidate this quote later in this chapter.

relation can only be a hostile one. In schizophrenia, on the other hand, there is no such re-cathexis of the object. The libido returns to autoerotism: "Dementia would correspond roughly to the success and paranoia to the failure of this return" (23F). For Freud, apparently, the return to autoerotism in schizophrenia implies a radical withdrawal from object-libido.

In Jung's reply to these letters, Freud's idea of a return of the libido to autoerotism is misunderstood. Jung agrees with Freud that there is a return to autoerotism in schizophrenia, but he interprets "autoerotism" in another way than Freud. Jung writes: "When you say that the libido withdraws from the object, you mean, I think, that it withdraws from the *real* object for normal reasons of repression (obstacles, unattainability, etc.) and throws itself on a phantasy copy of the real one, with which it then proceeds to play its classic autoerotic game" (24J). For Jung, the return to autoerotism is a withdrawal from reality into phantasy. But this was not what Freud had in mind. According to Freud, "the libido is not autoerotic as long as it has an object, *real or imagined.*" (25F, my emphasis) The withdrawal from the object implies a withdrawal from the *image* of the object. The withdrawal from reality is at the same time an internal catastrophe, because not only the relation to the real object is lost, but the image of the object in the subject is also eliminated. (Vandermeersch 1991)

This early misunderstanding between Freud and Jung is the first sign of their later disagreement, and implies a completely different conception of autoerotism and of its role in the mechanism of psychosis. This difference will in turn lead to two very different theories of psychosis and sexuality.

Jung on Psychosis and Sexuality

In 1911, Jung wrote *Symbols of Transformation,* (Jung 1956) in which he elaborates his intuition that the contents of psychotic delusions show a remarkable similarity with the themes of mythology, and presents his ideas about the nature of the unconscious and the libido. These ideas, however, move far away from Freud's psychoanalytic theory. The debate between Freud and Jung is a very complicated matter, both historically and theoretically. I will only indicate Jung's views on psychosis and sexuality in so far as they elucidate Freud's position on these matters by contrast.

According to Jung, psychotic delusions are characterised by intense *introversion*. Because of an actual frustration, the subject withdraws from reality into an inner world of phantasy. This introversion leads to a regression to an infantile phantasy-world. The phantasies evoke the blissful or frightening union of the child with the mother. However, according to Jung, this infantile regression is only a partial manifestation of a regression into the collective unconscious. According to Jung, the differences between human beings are the product of individuation and adaptation to different circumstances. The contents of the unconscious, however, are universal because the unconscious contains the remnants of the history and prehistory of the human race, including even its animal stages. In this way, we all share the same history, and the differences between you and me are only a late, ontogenetic, phenomenon. Therefore, the same archetypical images (the Hero, the Mother, etc.) dominate our unconscious.

This means that the images that dominate the phantasy-world of the psychotic cannot be interpreted in terms of the subject's personal history. In the last analysis, these phantasies are dominated by collective archetypes: "A person sinks into his childhood memories and vanishes from the existing world. He finds himself apparently in deepest darkness, but then has unexpected visions of a world beyond. The 'mystery' he beholds represents the stock of primordial images which everybody brings with him as his human birthright, the sum total of inborn forms peculiar to the instincts. I have called this 'potential' psyche the collective unconscious." (Jung 1956, 408) In this way, the psychotic can withdraw completely from reality: "For if the libido gets stuck in the wonderland of this inner world, then for the upper world man is nothing but a shadow, he is already moribund or at least seriously ill." (Jung 1956, 293) In this interpretation we recognise Jung's "misunderstanding" of Freud. Jung understands the withdrawal of libido as a withdrawal from reality into (collective) phantasy.

Jung's interpretation of libido-withdrawal as a return from reality to phantasy also leads to a new interpretation of libido. For Freud, libido was sexual libido, which must be distinguished from the ego-instincts. Freud is not a pan-sexualist because he is a dualist who maintained a radical distinction between sexuality and self-preservation. However, if libido is only sexual libido, how can a withdrawal of libido from real objects lead to a total loss of reality in psychosis? Would not the ego-instincts secure a strong enough tie with reality, even if we withdraw our sexual interest from real objects? Jung expresses this problem in a humoristic way: If Freud is right that the loss of reality results from the withdrawal of sexual interest, then there would be no difference between schizophrenia and sexual asceticism; after all, do not both the schizophrenic and the ascetic anchorite withdraw their sexual interest from reality?

According to Jung, therefore, the possibility of a *total* loss of reality in psychosis reveals that the libido comprises not only sexual interest but interest *in general*.[5] If the schizophrenic loses all interest in the outer world, he must have withdrawn all *types* of interest, and not just sexual interest. According to Jung, "we would be better advised, therefore, when speaking of libido, to understand

---

5   "It can hardly be supposed that the normal *fonction du réel*, to use Janet's term, is maintained only through affluxes of libido or erotic interest. The fact is that in very many cases reality disappears entirely, so that the patient shows no trace of psychological adaptation. (In these states, reality has been buried under the contents of the unconscious.) One is compelled to admit that not only the erotic interest, but all interest whatsoever, has completely disappeared except for a few feeble flickers, and with it the man's whole relation to reality." (Jung 1956, 134)

it as an energy-value which is able to communicate itself to any field of activity whatsoever, be it power, hunger, hatred, sexuality, or religion, without ever being itself a specific instinct." (Jung 1956, 137)

Jung's interpretation of libido as a general psychic energy destroys the fundaments of Freud's theory of infantile sexuality. What for Freud were the manifestations of infantile sexuality are for Jung not sexual at all. According to Jung, thumb-sucking derives from the act of nutrition. The fact that thumb-sucking becomes independent of the satisfaction of hunger does not make it a sexual activity; it only means that sucking is taken up in a *rhythmical* activity, which can now be displaced to other regions of the body.[6] When this rhythmical activity is displaced onto the sexual organs, it will lead to infantile masturbation. In this way, the libido will gradually develop into sexual libido and eventually into all the different interests of adult life. In psychosis, says Jung, there is a regression, not to infantile sexuality, but to the pre-sexual phase, in which hunger and rhythmical activities were the only manifestations of the libido. (Jung 1956, 144-145)

Jung's libido-theory therefore implies that regressions to childhood must not be interpreted as a return to infantile sexuality. For Freud, our phantasies and dreams are dominated by incestuous sexual wish-impulses. In this, according to Jung, Freud is misled by his hysterical patients. Incestuous phantasies are products of later phases of development. They accompany the regression of the libido and sexualise the memories of childhood, so that the sexual phantasies of the adult are projected back into childhood. This is the reason why the childhood memories of hysterics abound in seductions and other sexual scenes; the memories are distorted by later sexual phantasies. The adult is thus afraid to sink into his childhood memories, because *from the perspective of the adult* the tender relation with the mother is incestuous.

According to Jung, however, the mother is the symbol of the collective unconscious.[7] The regressions in psychosis reveal a return to the pre-sexual relation between the mother and the child. The sexual metaphors of hysterical regression change in psychosis into metaphors derived from the nutritive and digestive functions. Furthermore, these metaphors are only a *façon de parler*. (Jung 1956, 419) Actually, the regressions are directed towards the collective psyche, and the regression to infancy is only a way to clothe the collective archetypes in the language of personal psychology.[8]

---

[6] "Sucking still belongs to the sphere of the nutritive function, but outgrows it by ceasing to be a function of nutrition and becoming an analogous rhythmic activity without intake of nourishment." (Jung 1956, 144)

[7] The regressions to childhood memories "reawaken the relationship to the mother, *and so to something older than the mother.*" (1956, 334, my emphasis)

[8] "What actually happens in these incest and womb phantasies is that the libido immerses itself in the unconscious, thereby provoking infantile reactions, affects, opinions and attitudes from the personal sphere, but at the same time activating collective images (archetypes) which have a compensatory and curative meaning such as has always pertained to the myth." (Jung 1956, 420)

What appeared as a misunderstanding in April 1907, thus subsequently became the germ of a radically different conception of psychosis and sexuality.

Freud on Psychosis and Sexuality

Freud's works between 1910 and 1920 can be read as one long debate with Jung on the problem of psychosis and sexuality.

In 1911, Freud wrote his *Psychoanalytic Notes on an Autobiographical Account of a Case of Paranoia*. In this work, Freud wanted to show that what he had discovered in the therapy of the neuroses could be applied in the case of psychosis as well.[9] Freud never met Daniël Schreber. Freud based his analysis on Schreber's book, *Memoirs of My Nervous Illness*, (Schreber 2000) in which he describes how he experienced two subsequent nervous breakdowns.

During his first hospitalisation, Schreber suffered from severe hypochondria. He recovered within one year and there followed eight years of happiness and success. Schreber and his wife were only disappointed in their wish to have children. However, at the time Schreber was appointed Senatspräsident, he had some dreams indicating that he would become ill again. Once, in half-sleep, the idea came to him that it would be "very nice to be a woman submitting to the act of copulation." (Freud 1911, 13) A few weeks later, the second illness set in. But now his hypochondria was accompanied by delusional ideas that his brain was growing soft, that he would soon be dead or that he was already dead and decomposing, that "his body was being handled in all kinds of revolting ways", that the world had come to an end, etc. He also had the delusional idea that he was being persecuted and injured, especially by doctor Flechsig, his physician. (1911, 14) After a while, however, these delusions developed into a delusional *system*: Schreber thought that he had to save the world and that in order to do so, he had to be transformed into a woman. (1911, 16) This "systematisation" of his delusions enabled him at the same time to lead a fairly normal life apart from these ideas. (1911, 15)

Freud's presupposition is that the content of psychotic delusions is the same as the contents of neurotic conflict.[10] Indeed, Freud describes Schreber's paranoia as a defence against a sexual impulse. According to Freud, Schreber repressed his homosexual impulses towards his physician, Doctor Flechsig. (1911, 43) Schreber's dreams that he would become ill again express the wish to see Flechsig again. (1911, 42) When Schreber had the idea that it would be a

---

[9] "We have only to follow our usual psychoanalytic technique." (Freud 1911, 35)
[10] "The psychoanalyst, in the light of his knowledge of the psychoneuroses, approaches the subject with the suspicion that even thought-structures so extraordinary as these and so remote from our common modes of thinking are nevertheless derived from the most general and comprehensible impulses of the human mind." (1911, 18)

pleasure to enjoy sex as a woman, "this idea was one which he would have rejected with the greatest indignation if he had been fully conscious." (1911, 13)

Up to this point, Freud describes Schreber's problem as a neurotic conflict, and in this way, he holds on to an idea he already expressed in his correspondence with Fliess: paranoia is a neurosis of defence. Schreber repressed his homosexual impulse towards Flechsig, but the repressed returned in the form of a delusion of persecution. Schreber fears that Flechsig will rape and destroy him. In his study of Schreber, Freud explains how the repression of a homosexual impulse can lead to a delusion of persecution. The homosexual impulse, *I love him*, is contradicted: *I do not love him—I hate him*. What is specific to paranoia, according to Freud, is the fact that this protest too cannot become conscious to the paranoiac. Only the projected form, *He hates me*, can enter consciousness. (1911, 63) In this way, Schreber's homosexual attitude towards Flechsig is repressed and returns in the fear of being raped by Flechsig. However, Freud does not explain why the intermediate phase, *I hate him*, cannot become conscious in paranoia.

His interpretation also leads to another problem. The delusion of persecution is not the only delusion Schreber suffers from. When Schreber fears that he will be raped by Flechsig, or that he must have sex with God, the repressed homosexual impulse clearly returns. However, in his *Memoirs*, the delusion of the end of the world plays an equally important part.[11] It is hard to see how this "observation" that the world has come to an end is a projection of a repressed homosexual impulse.

Confronted with this delusion, then, it begins to dawn on Freud that his conceptualisation of neurosis fails in the case of psychosis. At the end of his study of Schreber, Freud says that the delusion of the end of the world is a projection of an "internal catastrophe." (1911, 70) But what is this internal catastrophe? To explain it, Freud returns to the idea of libido-withdrawal he already expressed in letters 22F and 23F to Jung: "His subjective world has come to an end since his withdrawal of his love from it." (1911, 70) According to Freud, the withdrawal of libido is not just a withdrawal of libido from real objects, but also an elimination of their representations within the subject. In *The Unconscious* (1915) and in *A Metapsychological Supplement to the Theory of Dreams* (1917 [1915]), Freud will give a more technical description of this "internal catastrophe". In *The Unconscious*, Freud explicitly states that the defence in psychosis cannot be understood as a repression.[12] In schizophrenia, the libido withdraws *from the unconscious*. (1917, 235) In this way, the psychotic elimination of a wish-impulse differs from its repression, which is the withdrawal of libido from the pre-conscious.

---

[11] Schreber 2000, passim. See also: Vergote 1998, 226.

[12] "A doubt must occur to us whether the process here termed repression has anything at all in common with the repression which takes place in the transference neuroses." (1915, 203)

It is only from this perspective of a withdrawal *from* the unconscious that we can understand why the protest against the homosexual wish-impulse (*I do not love him—I hate him*) could not enter consciousness. The protest against the wish-impulse could not become conscious because the impulse is *abolished* in the unconscious. Freud seems to be aware that this idea of a withdrawal of the libido from the unconscious opens a whole new perspective upon psychosis: "It was incorrect to say that the perception which was *suppressed* internally is *projected* outwards; the truth is rather, as we now see, that what was *abolished* internally *returns from without*."(1911, 71, my emphasis) In this description, Freud distinguishes psychosis from neurosis. Only what is internally eliminated, and not just repressed and preserved in the unconscious, can return from without. What is "projected" is a psychic catastrophe, not a repressed wish-impulse.[13] According to Jung, the psychotic withdraws from reality into phantasy. According to Freud, the withdrawal from reality *and* phantasy results in an internal catastrophe. The sexual phantasy, which enables the other to appear as another me, is abolished. In the case of Schreber, the real object (Flechsig) is lost because the image of the object in the subject is lost. Psychosis reveals a (partial) destruction of phantasy. The other cannot appear as "another me" anymore.

This conception of psychosis implies, therefore, that Freud's idea that paranoia is the result of a projection of repressed homosexuality cannot be maintained. Psychosis does not involve a repression of a homosexual phantasy, but rather a destruction of the monosexual, reflexive phantasies that are characteristic of homosexuality, sadomasochism, and scopophilia. *Because of this destruction, the other can only appear as a terrifying figure, which is no longer an actor in my scenario.*

The attempt to re-establish the other as "another me" necessarily fails. This also explains Freud's idea that the delusions of paranoia are an attempt at recovery. The feeling of being persecuted by an object is a way to re-establish a relation to a real object. When Schreber creates the delusion that Flechsig wants to rape and destroy him, he has of course a very intense relation to an object. But this relation can only be one of hostility.[14] This does not mean that Schreber's tender feelings for Flechsig are *transformed* into hostile feelings. Schreber's relation to Flechsig was first *abolished* internally. The hostile relation, therefore, is not just a change of the relation, but first of all a way to *re-establish* a relation.[15]

---

[13] This intuition is elaborated by W. Bion: "The spectacle presented is one, to borrow Freud's analogy, similar to that of the archaeologist who discovers in his field-work the evidences, not so much of primitive civilization, as of a primitive catastrophe." (Bion 1967, 88)

[14] "The human subject has recaptured a relation, and often a very intense one, to the people and things in the world, even though the relation is a hostile one now, where formerly it was hopefully affectionate." (1911, 71)

[15] "The libido *returns to its object*, tries to prevail, and with a *reversal to unpleasure* clings to the perceptions into which the object has been transformed." (McGuire 1974, 22F, my emphasis)

This is highlighted by the fact that Schreber's delusional system enables him to lead a "normal" life again. In the phase of his illness when he thought he was dead and decomposing, on the other hand, "the patient was so much pre-occupied with these pathological experiences that he was inaccessible to any other impression and would sit perfectly rigid and motionless for hours (hallucinatory stupor)." (1911, 14)

For Jung too, psychosis is an attempt at recovery. The psychotic withdraws into the collective unconscious to discover the imagos that are concerned with the actual problem. However, Freud's idea of the attempt at recovery in psychosis is completely different. It necessarily fails because the attempt to re-cathect an object only reaches the word-representations of the object.[16] Schreber's delusions about Flechsig never re-establish an affective relation to the real Flechsig. This does not mean that the psychotic delusions and hallucinations are a return to an imaginary world, however; they are instead an attempt to build a new relation to the world which "then find[s itself] obliged to be content with words instead of things." (1915, 204)

Narcissism and Dualism

In *On Narcissism: An Introduction* (1914), Freud also addresses Jung's idea that the libido must be considered as a general psychic energy and not as *libido sexualis*. As we have seen, Jung's libido-concept was the result of his conception of psychosis and of his work with psychotic patients in whose regressions sexuality did not seem to play a dominant role. In his critique of Jung, Freud only stresses that sexuality must not be understood phenomenologically, but biologically.[17] What is sexual and what is not, can only be determined by biology.

Freud's Darwinist perspective implies that every pleasure beyond the satisfaction of a vital need is therefore a sexual pleasure. This is the reason why, for Freud, Jung's "pre-sexual phase" is sexual after all. Thumb-sucking reveals that sucking the mother's breast was not only motivated by hunger, but also by a search for pleasure that later became independent of hunger in

---

[16] "It turns out that the cathexis of the word-presentation is not part of the act of repression, but represents the first of the attempts at recovery or cure which so conspicuously dominate the clinical picture of schizophrenia. These endeavours are directed towards regaining the lost object, and it may well be that to achieve this purpose they set off on a path that leads to the object via the verbal part of it, but then find themselves obliged to be content with words instead of things." (1915, 203)

[17] "I should like at this point expressly to admit that the hypothesis of separate ego-instincts and sexual instincts (that is to say, the libido-theory) rests scarcely at all upon a psychological basis, but derives its principal support from biology." (Freud 1914, 79)

thumb-sucking: "The first autoerotic sexual satisfactions are experienced in connection with vital functions which serve the purpose of self-preservation. The sexual instincts are at the outset attached to the satisfaction of the ego-instincts; only later do they become independent of these." (1914, 87) Freud's reply to Jung's critique is a very theoretical one. In the infant's relation to the mother, the difference between the sexual and the ego-instincts cannot be *observed* because, at this stage, pleasure remains attached to the satisfaction of vital needs. However, that does not mean that the difference between sexual and ego-instincts does not *exist* in this phase.

5. Love and Need in *Instincts and their Vicissitudes* (1915)

In the previous chapters, we have seen how, between 1905 and 1915, Freud elaborated a theory of sexual phantasy and object-choice. In *Instincts and their Vicissitudes* (1915), he finally solved the problem of sadomasochism he had left unanswered in the *Three Essays* (1905). Masochistic pleasure is possible because of the sadomasochistic phantasy, which originated in a sadistic pleasure turned around upon itself. However, *Instincts and their Vicissitudes* (1915) does not only deal with the problem of sexual perversion. It was meant to be a conclusive treatment of the Freudian theory of the instincts. But in fact it raised a lot of new problems that would lead Freud to a radical revision of his theory of the instincts in *Beyond the Pleasure Principle* (1920). In *Instincts*, Freud introduced the problems of pain, aggression and hate in relation to the *ego-instincts*. In this chapter, we will show that these problems could not be solved within Freud's theory at that time.

In the first pages of his paper, Freud defines his concept of "instinct". First of all, he distinguishes an instinct from an impulse. When a strong light falls on our eyes, we close our eyes. The flight from the stimulus happens as a reflex movement. This is possible because the impulse comes from outside the organism. An instinct, on the other hand, comes from within. Freud's examples, hunger and thirst, require a complicated action to remove the stimulus. Freud then goes on to describe the effect of instincts on "an almost entirely helpless living organism, as yet unorientated in the world." (1915, 119) According to Freud, the human infant, which is unable to perform the adequate actions to satisfy its needs, experiences the instinctual demands as something against which flight is to no avail. Originally, the instincts are *something one simply cannot get rid of.*[1]

These introductory remarks show that in *Instincts and their Vicissitudes*, Freud presents a somewhat different conception of the instinct from that which he presented in 1905. In the *Three Essays* (1905), Freud's concept of instinct was modelled upon the sexual instinct. Its only real aim was the search for pleasure. In *Jokes and their Relation to the Unconscious* (1905), Freud described the psyche as a pure pleasure-machine: "If we do not require our mental apparatus at the moment for supplying one of our indispensable satisfactions, we allow it itself to work in the direction of pleasure and we seek to derive pleasure from its own activity." (1905, 95) This is the way in which

---

[1] "We thus arrive at the essential nature of instincts in the first place by considering their main characteristics—their origin in sources of stimulation within the organism and their appearance as a constant force—and from this we deduce one of their further features, namely, that *no actions of flight avail against them.*" (1915, 119, my emphasis)

Freud describes the dominance of the pleasure principle. The mental apparatus works in the direction of pleasure.

In *Instincts* (1915), however, Freud's first examples of instincts are the ego-instincts (thirst and hunger).² Freud's new emphasis on the ego-instincts leads to a shift in his formulation of the pleasure principle. In 1915, Freud says, "The nervous system is an apparatus which has the function of getting rid of the stimuli that reach it, or of reducing them to the lowest possible level." (1915, 120) Of course, this is still the pleasure principle, because according to the pleasure principle "the whole of psychical activity is aimed at avoiding unpleasure and procuring pleasure." (Laplanche & Pontalis 1988, 322) But in the formulation of 1915 the emphasis has shifted *from the search for pleasure to the avoidance of unpleasure*. Between 1905 and 1915, there appears a shift of emphasis in the formulation of the pleasure principle and, in my opinion, this shift is caused by the fact that Freud introduces the analysis of the ego-instincts.

However, there are *two* groups of primal instincts: the sexual instincts and the ego-instincts. Freud emphasises again that this dualistic theory of the instincts is not based on clinical observation. It is a hypothesis based on biology: "I am altogether doubtful whether any decisive pointers for the differentiation and classification of the instincts can be arrived at on the basis of working over the psychological material." (1915, 124) However, clinical observation shows that both these instincts have different vicissitudes. Those of the sexual instincts can be observed in the psychoanalysis of the neuroses. According to Freud, it should be possible for the psychoanalysis of psychosis to analyse the ego-instincts.³

Freud then begins to describe the vicissitudes of the sexual instincts. These sexual instincts are still (as in 1905) motivated by the search for pleasure. When Freud says that this pleasure is an *organ*-pleasure, he stresses the fact that, for the sexual instincts, the object is highly unimportant. (1915, 125-6) The sexual instincts are pleasure-seeking, not object-seeking. The body wants pleasure and the qualities of the object do not matter as long as it provides pleasure. This characteristic of the sexual instincts is crucial. It explains why the loss of the object (the absence of the mother) does not affect them. Sucking the mother's breast, for instance, satisfies hunger and provides organ-pleasure. However, in the absence of the mother, the sexual instinct becomes autoerotic in thumb-sucking. This move from "allo-erotic" to autoerotic pleasure is possible because the sexual instinct is only interested in pleasure, not in the object that provides it.

[2] "For example, when a strong light falls on the eye, it is not an instinctual stimulus; it is one, however, when a dryness of the mucous membrane of the pharynx or an irritation of the mucous membrane of the stomach makes itself felt." (1915, 118)
[3] "With the extension of psychoanalysis to the other neurotic affections [the psychoses], we shall no doubt find a basis for our knowledge of the ego-instincts as well." (1915, 124)

Freud then analyses this movement from allo- to autoerotic pleasure in the case of sadism and voyeurism. According to Freud, the sexual instincts deal with the loss of the object in the following way (1915, 127):

(a) Sadism consists in the exercise of violence or power upon some other person as object.
(b) This object is given up and replaced by the subject's self.

The same is true of voyeurism (1915, 129):

(a) Looking as an activity directed towards an extraneous object.
(b) Giving up of the object and turning of the scopophilic instinct towards a part of the subject's own body.

In the previous chapter, we discussed the fact that this turn to reflexivity in the instinct is narcissistic, rather than autoerotic. But this difference is not important here. The point is that the sexual instinct is able to overcome the loss of the object because it is only interested in pleasure. Violence against an object or violence against oneself provides the same pleasure.[4]

To understand the consequences of Freud's analysis of the sexual instincts in *Instincts*, let us imagine a subject who is dominated solely by the sexual instincts. The loss of the object would not destroy his pleasure; it would only make his instincts reflexive, and this would lead to a state in which the subject only loves himself. Towards the outer world, on the other hand, he would be completely indifferent.[5] This state would be primary

---

[4] However, there is another problem with Freud's analysis of the way the instinct becomes reflexive. Freud introduces Krafft-Ebing's terms for sexual perversions (sadism and voyeurism) when he speaks about aggressive behaviour or about looking at another person. In the general or biology-based sense of sexuality, this presents no problem; it merely means that there is pleasure in aggression and curiosity, so that "sadism" and "voyeurism" are used in a very broad sense. This leaves unsolved, however, the problem of how this "sadism" and this "voyeurism" can become the source of sadomasochism and scopophilia, as real sexual perversions. How does Freud maintain the connection between his analyses of the sexual instincts in terms of perversions and the sexual perversions as described by Krafft-Ebing? In *Instincts*, Freud seems to be aware of this problem, and he introduces a further complication into his analysis of voyeurism. Before the first phase (looking at an extraneous object), he suggests, there must have been an even earlier phase: "*Oneself looking at a sexual organ = a sexual organ being looked at by oneself.*" (1915, 130) In this phase the subject looks at his own *sexual* organ, and sexuality in a strict sense is introduced into the analysis of perversion. In 1915, however, Freud gives no arguments for the introduction of this phase. Only in 1923 will the phallic-oedipal organisation become a conceptually clarified part of Freud's sexual theory. Before *The Ego and the Id* (1923) and *The Infantile Genital Organization* (1923), the Oedipus and castration complexes are merely references to mythology; before 1923, in other words, Freud did not specify the status of infantile genital sexuality in his sexual theory.

[5] "If for the moment we define loving as the relation of the ego to its sources of pleasure, the situation in which the ego loves itself only and is indifferent to the external world illustrates the first of the opposites which we found to 'loving'

narcissism. According to Freud, however, such a phase of primary narcissism could never exist:[6] "In so far as the ego is autoerotic, it has no need of the external world, but, in consequence of *experiences undergone by the instincts of self-preservation*, it acquires objects from that world, and, in spite of everything, it cannot avoid feeling internal instinctual stimuli for the time as unpleasurable." (1915, 135, my emphasis) In the absence of the mother, the infant can satisfy its sexual instincts autoerotically, but the needs of the ego-instincts are not capable of autoerotic satisfaction because ego-instincts need real objects for their satisfaction. In this way, Freud makes a radical distinction between love and need.

According to Freud, we can only love what we enjoy. Therefore, our first love is self-love because the first thing we enjoy is our own autoerotic pleasure.[7] This connection between love and pleasure also implies that what we love cannot be identified with what we need. Freud emphasises that this distinction is expressed by language itself. We need protection, security, health, and so on, but we do not love these things because, in normal circumstances, we do not really *enjoy* them.[8] This distinction between love and need reflects the biologically founded dualism between the sexual instincts and the ego-instincts.[9] In *Instincts*, Freud does not analyse the ego-instincts as thoroughly as the sexual instincts. They only appear in his analysis of hatred: the frustration of the ego-instincts produces pain, and according to Freud, this pain is expelled from the ego. The painful part of the ego is projected in the external world, and pain is thus transformed into hatred against the external world.[10]

Freud's analysis of the difference between the sexual instincts and the ego-instincts has a peculiar consequence. Apparently, pleasure and pain have a different source. The sexual instincts are motivated by the search for pleasure, and are therefore able to survive the loss of the object because they can be satisfied autoerotically. In this state of primary narcissism, the opposite of love is not hate, but indifference. Pain, on the other hand, is the result of a

---

[love versus indifference]. In so far as the ego is autoerotic, it has no need of the external world." (1915, 135)

[6] According to Freud, primary narcissism is a state of the sexual instincts, not a phase in the development of the infant.

[7] "We define loving as the relation of the ego to its sources of pleasure." (1915, 135)

[8] "We do not say of objects which serve the interests of self-preservation that we *love* them; we emphasize the fact that we *need* them." (1915, 137)

[9] "The distinction between the ego-instincts and the sexual instincts which we have imposed upon our psychology is thus in conformity with the spirit of our language." (1915, 137)

[10] "For the pleasure-ego the external world is divided into a part that is pleasurable, which it has incorporated into itself, and a remainder that is extraneous to it. It has separated off a part of its own self, which it projects into the external world and feels as hostile." (1915, 136)

frustration of the ego-instincts. The loss of the object leaves the infant alone with a pain it cannot get rid of, and from this pain springs the hate of the object. According to Freud, "the true prototypes of the relation of hate are derived not from sexual life, but from the ego's struggle to preserve and maintain itself." (1915, 138)

This analysis of pain and hate, however, contradicts Freud's previous ideas about the pleasure principle. Freud had always considered pleasure and pain on the one hand, and love and hate on the other, to be dialectical opposites. The analysis of the ego-instincts, however, shows that pain and hate originate in the experiences undergone by the ego-instincts, while pleasure and love are connected to the sexual instincts. But then the relation between love and hate and between pleasure and pain must be described in a new way. We will now look briefly at each of these relations in turn.

1. *Love and hate*

In the analysis of a case of obsessional neurosis (1909), Freud discovered that the doubts, compulsions and rituals that are typical of obsessional neurosis must be traced back to a fundamental ambivalence between love and hate in the relation to an object. Normally, love conquers hate, or vice versa, but in the obsessional neurotic there is a "chronic co-existence of love and hatred." (1909, 239) According to Freud, this comes about when "somewhere in the prehistoric period of his infancy, the *two opposites should have been split apart* and one of them, usually the hatred, have been repressed." (1909, 239, my emphasis) This quote shows that in 1909 Freud thought of the relation of love and hate as one of dialectical opposites, in which one pole of the relation is the negative of the other. Hate implies the repression of love and vice versa, because both can be traced back to an original ambivalence where love and hate existed simultaneously.

In *Instincts and their Vicissitudes* (1915), however, Freud states that "hate, as a relation to objects, is older than love." (1915, 139) This implies that love and hate were not originally dialectical opposites. According to Freud, hate stems from the frustration of the ego-instincts, while love is related exclusively to the sexual instincts. To highlight the difference between 1909 and 1915, we will compare Freud's interpretations of the hatred that springs from a broken love relationship.

In 1909, Freud says, "[L]ove, if it is denied satisfaction, may easily be partly *converted* into hatred." (1909, 239, my emphasis) In 1915, however, he says, "[I]f a love-relation with a given object is broken off, hate not infrequently emerges in its place, so that *we get the impression of a transformation* of love into hate." (1915, 139, my emphasis) This impression is partly right and partly mistaken. It is right because to some extent, hate is "sadism", and as such it remains a negative love. In the anal-sadistic stage, love is expressed in the form of mastery, and is therefore hardly distinguishable from hate.[11] This implies that, by hating the former love-object, the subject can still derive erotic pleasure from the relation.[12] This regression to sadism shows that the sexual instinct is motivated purely by pleasure; the loss of the object in the case of a broken love-relation does not lead to frustration of the sexual instincts, but only to another way to obtain pleasure.

However, hate cannot be reduced to sadism: "It is also in part based on reactions of repudiation by the ego-instincts." (1915, 139) Hate is not just a negative form of love. Two forms of hate must be distinguished. On the one hand, there is an erotic form of hatred, which is a continuation of frustrated love. On the other hand, hate originates from the ego-instincts. When we love someone, we might also *need* him. In the relation of an infant with its mother, for instance, the child's pleasure is attached to the satisfaction of his vital needs. In such cases, the loss of the object provokes hate, and not just indifference. The sexual instinct will then "use" this hate in its search for pleasure.[13] In this way, the hate that sprang from the ego-instincts becomes a source of pleasure in sadism.

This analysis of hate contradicts Freud's earlier idea that love and hate are dialectically opposed: "They did not arise from the cleavage of any originally common entity, but sprang from different sources, and had each its own development before the influence of the pleasure-unpleasure relation made them into opposites." (1915, 138) According to Freud, love and hate only become opposites in genital love.[14] This idea of 'genital love' has raised a lot of confusion in psychoanalytic literature.

According to Laplanche and Pontalis, "genital love" expresses "the idea of a final form of sexuality—and even that of a 'completely normal attitude in love' which combines the trends of sensuality and 'affection' (*Zärtlichkeit*)". (Laplanche & Pontalis 1988, 185) Therefore, Laplanche and Pontalis are right to warn against the moralistic connotation of this term. One could wonder, however, whether this idea of genital love has not been misunderstood in the psychoanalytical tradition.[15] According to Freud, genital love has nothing to

---

[11] "At the higher stage of the pregenital sadistic-anal organization, the striving for the object appears in the form of an urge for mastery, to which injury and annihilation of the object is a matter of indifference. Love in this form and at this preliminary stage is hardly to be distinguished from hate towards the object." (1915, 138)

[12] "The hate, which has its real motives, is here reinforced by a regression of the love to the sadistic preliminary stage; so that the hate acquires an erotic character and the continuation of a love-relation is ensured." (1915, 139)

[13] "When the ego-instincts dominate the sexual function, as is the case at the stage of the sadistic-anal organization, they [the ego-instincts] impart the qualities of hate to the instinctual [sexual] aim as well." (1915, 139)

[14] "Not until the genital organization is established does love become the opposite of hate." (1915, 139)

[15] On Lacan's critique of Fairbairn's conception of genital love, see Van Haute 2002.

do with such moralistic definitions. Freud only stresses that, in genital pleasure, pleasure has become detached from the satisfaction of our vital needs. This implies that at the level of the genital organisation, we can *love* someone without *needing* him: "Thus the word 'to love' moves further and further into *the sphere of the pure pleasure-relation of the ego to the object* and finally becomes fixed to the sexual objects *in the narrower sense* and to those which satisfy the needs of sublimated sexual instincts." (1915, 137, my emphasis) Of course, this has nothing to do with maturity or normality, but with a state in which we only love what we enjoy but do not need. In this state, the absence of the object does not threaten our survival, but only our pleasure. In this interpretation of genital love, no warnings against moralism are needed, because genital love would be closer to pure hedonism than to a "normal" love-relation. It is a love without admixture of hate, because this love is based on the pure pleasure-relation alone.

2. *Pleasure and pain*

The pleasure-principle implies that "the whole of psychical activity is aimed at avoiding unpleasure and procuring pleasure". (Laplanche & Pontalis 1988, 322) However, Freud never clarified the difference between "avoiding unpleasure" and "procuring pleasure". To secure the idea of a psychical *economy*, he has to identify the search for pleasure with the avoidance of unpleasure. The economical perspective depends upon the idea that pleasure and unpleasure are a matter of more and less. "Unpleasure corresponds to an *increase* in the quantity of excitation and pleasure to a *diminution*." (1920, 8)

Phenomenologically, however, it is clear that when we experience pain, we do not experience it as a lack of pleasure. The Irish philosopher, Edmund Burke, already expressed this in a humoristic way: "Caius is afflicted with a fit of the cholic; this man is actually in pain; stretch Caius upon the rack, he will feel a much greater pain; but does this pain of the rack arise from the removal of any pleasure? Or is the fit of the cholic a pleasure or a pain just as we are pleased to consider it?" (Burke 1998, 81) According to Burke, "[P]ain and pleasure in their most simple and natural manner of affecting, are each of a positive nature, and by no means necessarily dependent on each other for their existence." (Burke 1998, 80)

Freud seems to suggest as much when he relates love and pleasure to the sexual instincts, and pain and hate to the experiences undergone by the ego-instincts. The pain that springs from the frustration of the ego-instincts is not the negative of pleasure (unpleasure). Here, pain is not a ceasing of pleasure; it has a positive nature. However, in 1915, Freud is not ready to question the pleasure principle, because this principle is the foundation of his idea of a psychical economy. This economic view of pleasure and pain always tempted Freud because it held the promise of a *scientific* psychology in which quality could be reduced to quantity. It is only in *Beyond the Pleasure-Principle*

(1920) that Freud will radically question the pleasure principle, and introduce a pain that has never been pleasure and cannot be analysed in terms of repressed pleasure or unpleasure.

The introduction of the ego-instincts brings Freud's metapsychology into question. In his study of Schreber (1911) and in *On Narcissism: An Introduction* (1914), Freud adhered to the idea that psychosis must be understood as a defence against a sexual impulse. In *Instincts and Their Vicissitudes* (1915), however, Freud said that the psychoanalysis of the psychoses would make possible the analysis of the ego-instincts. This seems to imply that the ego-instincts are not just well-adapted vital functions anymore; like the sexual instincts, they have their own pathological vicissitudes. The fact that Freud says that the analysis of psychosis will clarify the vicissitudes of the ego-instincts seems to mean that Freud comes closer to Jung. But for Freud, this does not mean that the dualism of the instincts should be abandoned; on the contrary, the different reactions of the ego-instincts and the sexual instincts to the loss of the object show the crucial difference between love and need.

In 1915, Freud introduces the ego-instincts in his analysis of hatred, but at the same time, he seems reluctant to elaborate on the consequences of this analysis. In *Beyond the Pleasure Principle* (1920), however, Freud will analyse the ego-instincts in a new way: "These guardians of life, too, were originally the myrmidons of death." (1920, 39) In *Beyond the Pleasure Principle*, Freud elaborates a new theory of the instincts, in which the different vicissitudes of the sexual instincts and the ego-instincts will be described not from the perspective of perversion and psychosis, but from the perspective of traumatic neurosis and infantile trauma.

6. The Capacity to Suffer

Freud's speculations on the death instinct in *Beyond the Pleasure Principle* (1920) have met with considerable resistance from many psychoanalysts. Only in Kleinian psychoanalysis has the death instinct become an important theoretical concept;[1] other analytic thinkers have been embarrassed by Freud's mythological biology of "death and Eros". However, Freud's reflections on the death instinct become very stimulating if they are interpreted as an analysis of traumatic neurosis translated into metaphors from biology. Only an attempt to "de-translate" Freud's biological speculations can clarify some of his most obscure formulations about death, self-preservation and sexuality. In *Inhibitions, Symptoms and Anxiety* (1926), Freud discusses the infantile traumas that are at the origin of the traumatic kernel of the unconscious. Only a confrontation of *Beyond the Pleasure Principle* with these clinical reflections about trauma elucidates the radical change of perspective in Freud's theory after 1920.

The compulsion to repeat

Before 1920, Freud interpreted negative affects such as disgust, shame and anxiety as repressed pleasures. This is expressed most clearly in his analyses of hysteric patients, where sexual disgust is a symptom of a repressed sexual desire. In the analysis of Dora (*Fragment of an Analysis of a Case of Hysteria*, 1905), Dora's nausea is analysed as the symptom of a repressed sexual phantasy of *fellatio*. (Freud 1905, 47) The same goes for obsessional neurosis. When another of Freud's patients, the Ratman, tells a story of rats eating their way into someone's anus, Freud notices how his patient's horror reveals a pleasure "of which he himself is unaware." (Freud 1909, 167) According to Freud, "there is no doubt that all neurotic unpleasure is of that kind—*pleasure that cannot be felt as such.*" (Freud 1920, 11, my emphasis)

The same idea of unpleasure as repressed pleasure underlies Freud's hypothesis that all dreams, even anxiety-dreams, are wish fulfilments. In *The Interpretation of Dreams* (1900), Freud analysed the recurring nightmare of one of his patients. At the beginning of puberty this man used to dream that a man was pursuing him with a hatchet. He would try to escape but feel as if he was paralysed. In the associations to this dream, the patient connected the dream scene to his brother and the fights they had together: "He particularly

---

[1] Klein's concept of the death instinct, however, differs in essential aspects from Freud's. (Cf. Geyskens & Van Haute 2003)

remembered an occasion when he [the patient] had kicked him [the brother] on the head with his boot and had drawn blood, and how his mother had said: 'I'm afraid he'll be the death of him one day'." (Freud 1900, 584)

This association then brought on another, earlier one. When the patient was nine years old, he had overheard his parents making love. Apparently, he had associated this with his violent, bloody fights with his brother: "He had found evidence in favour of this view in the fact that he had often noticed blood in his mother's bed." (Freud 1900, 585) These interconnected memories had found a representation in his anxiety-dream of a man pursuing him with a hatchet.

Freud then asked himself what was the source of anxiety in this dream. According to Freud, the dream was motivated by the *sexual excitation* the patient had experienced when he overheard his parents making love. This memory, however, was repressed because it involved the parents' sexual life, and the manifest dream-content therefore only represented this memory in a distorted manner. The anxiety provoked by this dream, however, is that sexual excitation, transformed into anxiety because of repression. The dream is a wish fulfilment, the expression of a sexual excitation, but because of repression, the affect that accompanies this dream is anxiety instead of pleasure.

This analysis of anxiety as transformed libido implies that "if the course of ideas in the Ucs. were left to itself, it would generate an affect which was originally of a pleasurable nature, but became unpleasurable after the process of 'repression' occurred." (Freud 1900, 582) The anxiety was not originally provoked by the fear of the man with the hatchet; it became attached to it in the manifest dream-content retrospectively.[2] Originally the anxiety was sexual excitation transformed into anxiety.

However, analytic experience taught Freud that not every negative affect could be explained in this way, a fact that Freud discovered in his analysis of the war neuroses. During the First World War, soldiers who returned from the front showed peculiar, neurotic symptoms: they were incapable of moving about, the attempt to move caused violent tremors of knees and feet, etc. (Ferenczi 1999, 129) It appeared that they were still haunted by the most horrible of their battlefield experiences. This was not because they dwelt on those experiences a great deal; in fact, they even tried not to think of them at all. But their dreams endlessly brought them back to scenes of horror.

These traumatic experiences were characterised not only by their violence, but even more the fact that they had come as a complete surprise; in other words, the patients had met the traumatic experiences with a lack of anxiety. Anxiety implies at least some degree of preparedness.[3] In severe traumatic

---

[2] "The anxiety had *taken over* the punishments with which he had been threatened earlier." (Freud 1900, 586, my emphasis)

[3] "'Anxiety' describes a particular state of expecting the danger or preparing for it, even though it may be an unknown one." (Freud 1920, 12)

situations, however, even anxiety fails, and this lack of anxiety was exactly what made these experiences traumatic. Only after the trauma had occurred did these patients suffer from anxiety attacks and recurring nightmares. According to Freud, these nightmares produce the anxiety that was impossible at the time of the trauma. Freud took a special interest in these nightmares because they contradicted his former theory that dreams, even anxiety-dreams, were wish fulfilments. The occurrence of these post-traumatic dreams is dominated rather by a compulsive repetition of the traumatic experience. Apparently, Freud concludes, there is a second function of dreams beside wish fulfilment. *The pain and the anxiety that were impossible at the time of the trauma, must be "suffered"*[4] *or subjectivised retrospectively,*[5] *and only when this has happened can dreams become wish fulfilment.*[6]

The discovery of this compulsion to repeat revealed that Freud's earlier theory of neurosis could not explain traumatic neurosis. The pain and the anxiety that characterise traumatic neurosis cannot be understood as "pleasure that cannot be felt as such" (Freud 1920, 11), for the traumatic experiences could not have produced pleasure in any way. Furthermore, the compulsion to repeat these traumatic experiences in dreams contradicts the idea that the mental apparatus is dominated exclusively by the search for pleasure and the avoidance of unpleasure. In their dreams, veterans repeated their most painful experiences again and again.

As such, however, this would not present a huge theoretical problem; it would only mean that traumatic neurosis must be distinguished from the other neuroses. But Freud goes further than this, suggesting that this second function of dreams (the binding of traumatic impressions by suffering the anxiety proper to them retrospectively) is actually their *original* function.[7] In *Beyond*

---

[4] "To suffer" must be understood, here, as an activity, and thus as different from "being affected by something". Bion already introduced this use of "to suffer" when he said that though the psychotic *feels* the pain, he is not able to *suffer* it: "The patients, for the treatment of whom I wish to formulate theories, experience pain but not suffering.... The *intensity* of the patient's pain contributes to his fear of suffering pain." (Bion 1970, 19)

[5] "According to Freud, we must consider that every repeated little traumata, the jump at every sudden noise or light, we should see as a tendency towards recovery, a tendency of the organism to re-establish the equilibrium disturbed by the distribution of tension throughout the organism." (Ferenczi 1999, 142)

[6] "The fulfilment of wishes is, as we know, brought about in a hallucinatory manner by dreams, and under the dominance of the pleasure principle this has become their function. But it is not in the service of that principle that the dreams of patients suffering from traumatic neuroses lead them back with such regularity to the situation in which the trauma occurred. We may assume, rather, that dreams are here helping to carry out another task, which must be accomplished before the dominance of the pleasure principle can even begin. These dreams are endeavouring to master the stimulus retrospectively, by developing the anxiety whose omission was the cause of the traumatic neurosis." (Freud 1920, 32)

[7] Freud says about dreams that "fulfilling the wishes of the disturbing impulses is not their *original* function." (Freud 1920, 33)

the Pleasure Principle, Freud says that the compulsion to repeat is not restricted to traumatic neurosis. All sorts of patients return again and again in analysis to experiences that could never have been pleasurable.[8] They always return to experiences that have mortified them, and thus "repeat all of these unwanted situations and painful emotions in the transference and revive them with the greatest ingenuity."[9]

In 1914, Freud had already written a paper on *Remembering, Repeating and Working-Through*. In this paper, he describes repetition in the transference as a peculiar form of resistance. Instead of remembering the repressed, patients act out what they cannot remember: "The patient does not *remember* anything of what he has forgotten and repressed, but *acts* it out. He reproduces it not as a memory but as an action; he *repeats* it, without, of course, knowing that he is repeating it." (Freud 1914, 150) In 1914, Freud describes this acting out as a technical problem; the analyst must try to limit the acting out of his patient and enable him to remember instead. At the same time, the analyst must know that a complete replacement of repeating by remembering cannot be accomplished.[10]

In *Beyond the Pleasure Principle* (1920), Freud takes up this problem of acting out again, and by then, Freud has realised that this acting out is not just a form of resistance. The repetition of traumatic experiences is a more general phenomenon, of which the acting out in the transference is only one example. Acting out reveals the same compulsion to repeat that Freud discovered in the war neuroses. In both cases, the original function of this compulsion to repeat is to suffer the traumatic experiences retrospectively in order to subjectivise them.

Acting out can be interpreted as a resistance to remembering. The patient makes the analyst behave towards him in an inconsiderate and cold manner because it is too painful to elaborate on the inconsiderateness of his parents during childhood. Viewed in this way, acting out is in the service of the pleasure principle.[11] However, there is another dimension to acting out that this

---

[8] "The compulsion to repeat also recalls from the past experiences which include no possibility of pleasure, and which can never, even long ago, have brought satisfaction even to instinctual impulses which have since been repressed." (Freud 1920, 20)

[9] "They seek to bring about the interruption of the treatment while it is still incomplete; they contrive once more to feel themselves scorned, to oblige the physician to speak severely to them and treat them coldly; they discover appropriate objects of their jealousy; instead of the passionately desired baby of their childhood, they produce a plan or a promise of some grand present—which turns out as a rule to be no less unreal." (Freud 1920, 21)

[10] "Remembering in the old manner—reproduction in the psychical field—is the aim to which he adheres, even though he knows that such an aim cannot be achieved in the new technique." (Freud 1914, 153)

[11] "The compulsion to repeat, which the treatment tries to bring into its service is, as it were, drawn over by the ego to its side (clinging as the ego does to the pleasure principle)." (Freud 1920, 23)

interpretation misses: the fact that by repeating painful experiences from the past, the patient is able to "suffer" these experiences for the first time. Sandor Ferenczi, one of the earliest followers of Freud, says in his article on war neuroses, *Two Types of War Neuroses* (1916): "[Sufferers of these neuroses] have the compulsion to expose themselves anew to similar experiences as though they were trying to control the originally unconscious and uncomprehended experience by a subsequent conscious one." (Ferenczi 1999, 143) During analysis, however, this compulsion to repeat can operate in the service of the pleasure principle: "The phenomena of transference are obviously exploited by the resistance which the ego maintains in its pertinacious insistence upon repression." (Freud 1920, 23) It is still true for Freud in 1920, as it was in 1914, that repetition is a resistance to remembering, but Freud no longer considers this the original function of the compulsion to repeat. The compulsion to repeat can be motivated by the avoidance of unpleasure, but originally it had another function: "suffering" traumatic experiences retrospectively.

Freud emphasises this double register of the compulsion to repeat in his analysis of a game played by his grandson, who was in the habit of taking small objects and throwing them away, accompanying every throw with the exclamation "O-o-o-o," which apparently meant "Gone" [*Fort*]. Freud interprets this game as follows. The child was a "good boy" who was very attached to his mother, very obedient and "not at all precocious in his intellectual development." (Freud 1920, 14) On occasions when his mother left him alone for a time, he never cried. But just because he did not protest against his mother leaving him alone does not mean that he did not mind her absence. On the contrary, "he was overpowered by the experience." (Freud 1920, 16) The boy did not cry because he was too overwhelmed to take a subjective position towards his experience; he was unable to react with anger, anxiety or sadness, and instead actively repeated the experience of loss.

This repetition could not have been motivated by the search for pleasure or the avoidance of unpleasure, because the loss of the mother was a painful experience, and there was no pleasure to be gained by repeating it. Neither was the repetition just an automatic return of the same, however. In the original situation, the infant was in a completely passive position; by actively repeating the trauma, he gained an active position towards it. This active position must not be understood as a position of mastery; it merely means that the child was subsequently able to react with anger or anxiety to the absence of the mother, which was impossible at the time of the trauma.

Only when this capacity to suffer was established could the child also derive pleasure from his game. For instance, throwing away objects might signify that he was revenging himself on his mother for going away, and in this way, the compulsion to repeat might be drawn over to the side of the pleasure principle. Freud's point in *Beyond the Pleasure Principle* is simply that obtaining pleasure or avoiding unpleasure is not the original function of the compulsion to repeat, and the same is true of the transference in the analytic cure.

A Death Instinct?

According to Freud, the compulsion to repeat gives the impression of being something instinctual or "daemonic".[12] Freud gives the example of a woman who married three times and whose husbands all fell ill shortly after the wedding and "had to be nursed by her on their death-beds." (Freud 1920, 22) What is most remarkable, however, is that Freud sees this daemonic force at work not only in such extreme examples, but also in the analytic cure and in the infantile psyche. This implies that for Freud the compulsion to repeat is not a marginal phenomenon; it is the most original force at work in mental life. But what does it mean when he calls this mysterious force "instinctual" [*Triebhaft*]?

When Freud introduced the sexual and the ego-instincts, he explicitly referred to the biological notion of "instinct". However, when Freud says that phenomena that are dominated by the compulsion to repeat give an appearance of being instinctual, there is no such reference to biology. In *Beyond the Pleasure Principle*, Freud invents his own biology and introduces a whole new notion of "instinct": "An instinct is an urge inherent in organic life to restore an earlier state of things which the living entity has been obliged to abandon under the pressure of external disturbing forces." (Freud 1920, 36) Neither Darwin nor any other biologist ever defined the concept of "instinct" in this way.

On closer examination, Freud's definition of "instinct" is only a description of the compulsion to repeat, reformulated in metaphors from biology. Indeed, the war veterans repeated their traumas in their dreams in order "to restore an earlier state of things" which they had "been obliged to abandon under the pressure of external disturbing forces". In this way, traumatic neurosis becomes the paradigm in Freud's speculation about the origin of life. According to Freud, all the phenomena of life are the compulsive repetition of an original trauma.[13] The instinct, then, is the tendency to get rid of the tension produced by this original upheaval: "The tension which then arose in what had hitherto been an inanimate substance endeavoured to cancel itself out. In this way the first instinct came into being." (Freud 1920, 38)

From this perspective, it becomes clear why Freud says that the aim of life is death. (Freud 1920, 38) If life is nothing but the tension provoked by an original "trauma" and the compulsive repetition of this trauma, the tendency

---

[12] "The manifestations of a compulsion to repeat (which we have described as occurring in the early activities of infantile mental life as well as among the events of psychoanalytic treatment) exhibit to a high degree an instinctual character and, when they act in opposition to the pleasure principle, give the appearance of some 'daemonic' force at work." (Freud 1920, 35)

[13] "The attributes of life were at some time evoked in inanimate matter by the action of a force of whose nature we can form no conception." (Freud 1920, 38)

of life can only be a tendency "to cancel itself out." (Freud 1920, 38) Freud's mythical biology seems to be based on the idea that the inorganic world received a shock from which it has to recover. Life, then, is the inorganic's attempt at recovery. Biologically, this is of course sheer nonsense. Freud's speculations in *Beyond the Pleasure Principle* only make sense as reflections on clinical phenomena. In the context of the war neuroses, it is clear that the compulsion to repeat is motivated by a tension that wants to cancel itself out. The compulsion to repeat is an attempt to get rid of the tension produced by the trauma.

Freud hardly mentions the death instinct in his later clinical works, in *Inhibitions, Symptoms and Anxiety* (1926), *Fetishism* (1927), *Splitting of the Ego in the Process of Defence* (1938), and in the analysis of neurosis in *Moses and Monotheism* (1939). But in these works, he develops a theory of neurosis that is centred on the idea of an infantile trauma and its compulsive repetition. This shows that for Freud the compulsion to repeat an infantile trauma is the clinical manifestation of the death instinct. Freud's biological metaphors only obscure his new discovery: dreams and symptoms have a more original function than wish fulfilment. They are attempts to recover from an infantile trauma.[14]

Freud's notion of a death instinct, however, enabled him to reformulate his former dualism between the sexual instincts and the instincts of self-preservation in a new way. The instincts of self-preservation lose much of their significance now that Freud defines the instinct as a tendency towards death. Apparently, the instincts of self-preservation do not want to preserve life at all costs. Their only function remains "to assure that the organism shall follow its own path to death, and to ward off any possible ways of returning to inorganic existence other than those which are immanent in the organism itself." (Freud 1920, 39) What does this obscure passage mean?

To understand Freud's argument, we have to translate the biological metaphors and discover the clinical phenomena of traumatic neurosis behind them. If the aim of all life is death, it is not hard to imagine a short way to reach this aim: suicide. However, it is a remarkable fact that in traumatic neuroses suicide is rare (Green 2000a, 142). It is rather the case that the compulsion to repeat the trauma paralyses mental life.[15] What follows is a slow "mortification", not suicide. It is also the case that these people do not lose the normal fear of external dangers. When some of them live dangerous lives, they are only involved in dangers that must be considered repetitions of the trauma, and not merely accidents.[16]

---

[14] This idea is further developed by Ferenczi. (Ferenczi 1982, 141-2)
[15] "An 'anticathexis' on a grand scale is set up, for whose benefit all the other psychical systems are impoverished, so that the remaining psychical functions are extensively paralysed or reduced." (Freud 1920, 30)
[16] "The organism wishes to die only in its own fashion" (Freud 1920, 39).

In *The Deer Hunter*, for instance, a soldier witnesses a game of Russian roulette, but is unable to react. Later, however, he starts to play the game himself. This is not an indication that he wants to commit suicide; it shows, rather, that only the compulsion to repeat the trauma eventually leads him to his own death. The active repetition of the trauma is an attempt to "suffer" it, and thereby to recover from it. The "daemonic" appearance of this repetition is due to the fact that it is always a *failed* attempt at recovery.[17] It is only from the perspective of an objective spectator that the compulsion to repeat appears as a paradoxical attempt to kill oneself slowly: "Hence arises the paradoxical situation that the living organism struggles most energetically against events (dangers, in fact) which might help it to attain its life's aim rapidly—by a kind of short-circuit." (Freud 1920, 39) Freud understands the compulsion to repeat as a slow suicide; he does not see that it is also a failed attempt at recovery.

According to Freud, the function of the ego-instincts is only to "assure that the organism shall follow *its own* path to death." (Freud 1920, 39, my emphasis) This reveals the double register of the compulsion to repeat, which we already found in the game of Freud's grandson and in acting out. On the one hand, the compulsion to repeat leads to a continual return to the trauma, and in this way it endangers the life of the subject. On the other hand, however, it must also be understood as a resistance to the disappearance of the subject. In 1914, Freud conceived of the compulsion to repeat as a resistance to remembering (see above). In 1920, the compulsion to repeat is still a resistance, but it is no longer a resistance to remembering; the compulsion to repeat resists instead the pure trauma. If it did not repeat the trauma, the subject would be destroyed "by a kind of short-circuit." (Freud 1920, 39) The compulsion to repeat leads the subject into "*its own* path to death".

Our singularity as human subjects resides in a traumatic kernel we cannot get rid of. The compulsive repetition of this traumatic kernel, which is at the same time an attempt to recover from it, is what "singularises" us. The woman who nursed her three husbands on their deathbeds slowly sacrificed her life, but this suffering was exactly what made her life *her own* life. Thus, Freud can say, "We have no longer to reckon with the organism's puzzling determination (so hard to fit into any context) to maintain its own existence in the face of every obstacle. What we are left with is the fact that the organism wishes to die only in its own fashion." (Freud 1920, 39) This is of crucial importance for the analytic cure. If our singularity is essentially related to something traumatic and to its repetition in our symptoms and our destiny, it is clear that the aim of the cure cannot be to "free" us from our symptoms.

In our interpretation of *Beyond the Pleasure Principle*, we have switched from a few clinical phenomena to a theory with an anthropological claim. In doing this, we have followed Freud's text. In Freud's text too, the idea of a

---

[17] It is always a *failed* attempt because the "actual" trauma is itself a repetition of an infantile trauma. See below.

universal death instinct is based on a few examples (acting out, a child's game, and the compulsion to repeat a trauma). In *Beyond the Pleasure Principle*, however, Freud gives no arguments for this transition from pathology to anthropology or even to biology. For Freud, there seems to be an evident transition from the war traumas to a 'universal trauma.' But in *Beyond the Pleasure Principle* Freud does not specify what might be the universal trauma that is repeated throughout life, and neither does he explain why it can never be overcome. Six years after *Beyond the Pleasure Principle*, however, he discusses this problem in detail in *Inhibitions, Symptoms and Anxiety* (1926), where he returns to the problem of traumatic neurosis.

At first sight, it seems obvious what causes the war neuroses; traumatic neurosis often follows upon a narrow escape from death. According to Freud, however, the fear of death as such cannot provoke neurosis: "It would be highly improbable that a neurosis could come into being merely because of the objective presence of danger, without any participation of the deeper levels of the mental apparatus." (Freud 1926, 129) Freud's other argument against the fear of death—that death cannot provoke anxiety because there is no representation of death[18]—is highly unconvincing. Would the unrepresentability of death not rather enhance our anxiety? However, what Freud seems to have in mind is the idea that a narrow escape from death is as such not enough to explain the outbreak of a neurosis. A severe threat to life only provokes a traumatic neurosis because it brings us in a state of complete helplessness.

Unlike death, this helplessness is a situation we have all experienced when we were infants. When an infant is left alone by its mother, it will first hallucinate the mnemic image of her. (Freud 1926, 137) When this turns out to be ineffective, the infant starts to panic. Without its mother, it is helpless against its needs, which attack it from within[19]. The infant is left alone with a pain it cannot get rid of. This pain is not yet hunger, thirst, or any other specific need, which it will only learn how to deal with later on.[20] It is experienced as a

---

[18] "Nothing resembling death can ever have been experienced." (Freud 1926, 130)
[19] The idea that the infant hallucinates the image of the mother does not contradict the autoerotism of infantile sexuality. The ego-instincts always need an outer object. That is why the absence of an object leads to hallucination and to the failure of hallucination. The oral sexual instinct can be satisfied by thumbsucking. There is no need, here, for hallucination.
[20] "The reason why the infant in arms wants to perceive the presence of its mother is only because it already knows by experience that she satisfies all his needs without delay. The situation, then, which it regards as a 'danger' and against which it wants to be safeguarded is that of non-satisfaction, of a *growing tension due to need*, against which it is helpless." (Freud 1926, 137) This quote is a clear example of what Bowlby calls 'the theory of Secondary Drive'. Freud does not consider the domain of attachment and security as an original dimension of human existence. For Freud, the proximity of the mother is merely the guarantee of the satisfaction of the infant's vital needs (Bowlby 1969, 178). *Cf.* Geyskens & Van Haute (2003) and Geyskens (2003)

purely "economic disturbance caused by an accumulation of amounts of stimulation which require to be disposed of." (Freud 1926, 137) This purely biological helplessness is then replaced and overcome by a sense of psychical helplessness. The infant learns to consider the absence of the mother as such as a danger, even if its needs are satisfied. A situation of anxiety and pain is replaced by a situation of anxiety and the *anticipation* of pain. The infant does not need its mother now, but it might need her in the future.

According to Freud, "this change constitutes a first great step forward in the provision made by the infant for its self-preservation, and at the same time represents a transition from the automatic and involuntary fresh appearance of anxiety to the intentional reproduction of anxiety as a signal of danger." (Freud 1926, 138) This description of archaic danger-situations reveals the infantile factor in traumatic neurosis. Apparently, it is not the mortal danger as such, but the experience of radical passivity and helplessness, which we already experienced as infants, that is traumatic.[21] This passivity is the origin of the compulsion to repeat. The compulsive repetition will at the same time enable a "subjectivisation" of the trauma by actively repeating the experience of radical passivity.

This reference to an infantile trauma explains why Freud linked the ego-instincts to the death instinct. (Freud 1920, 44) The ego-instincts make us dependent and fragile, and because the infant needs its mother to satisfy its ego-instincts, the loss of the mother is traumatic. This mortification is at the origin of the compulsion to repeat. From then on, the ego-instincts are marked by a mortification they try to overcome. But does this make the ego-instincts into "component instincts" of the death instinct, as Freud would have it in *Beyond the Pleasure Principle*?[22]

The Indestructibility of the Sexual Instincts

So far, we have interpreted *Beyond the Pleasure Principle* from the perspective of the compulsive repetition of an original trauma. This interpretation is

---

[21] In *The Ego and the Id* (1923), Freud says, "When the ego finds itself in an excessive real danger which it believes itself unable to overcome by its own strength… it sees itself deserted by all protecting forces and lets itself die. Here, moreover, is once again the same situation as that which underlay the first great anxiety-state of birth and the infantile anxiety of longing—the anxiety due to separation from the protecting mother." (Freud 1923, 58) *Kamikaze* pilots did not shout the name of the Emperor when they crashed into American ships; they called for their mothers. The mortal dangers of adult life revive the archaic anxiety of losing the primal object.

[22] "Seen in this light, the theoretical importance of the instincts of self-preservation, of self-assertion and of mastery greatly diminishes. They are component instincts whose function it is to assure that the organism shall follow its own path to death." (Freud 1920, 39)

corroborated by Freud's analysis of the infantile anxiety-situations in *Inhibitions, Symptoms and Anxiety*. In *Inhibitions, Symptoms and Anxiety*, however, Freud does not mention the part played by the sexual instincts in these early anxiety-situations. How do sexual instincts react to the absence of the mother?

In *Beyond the Pleasure Principle*, Freud says that although the organism just wishes to die, some parts of the organism do not share this destiny. The germ cells enjoy what Freud calls a "potential immortality". (Freud 1920, 40) The germ cells are able to reproduce an organism that will produce the germ cells anew. Viewed from this perspective, the mortal individual is just a temporary carrier of the immortal germ cells. As such, however, this is just a biological fact. What has this to do with Freud's analysis of traumatic neurosis? This is a crucial question because for so long as it remains unanswered, Freud's speculations remain biological phantasies.

In *Instincts and their Vicissitudes* (1915), Freud analysed the different reactions of the ego-instincts and the sexual instincts to the loss of the object. In the absence of the mother, the ego-instincts of the infant cannot be satisfied. The sexual instincts, on the other hand, always survive the loss of the object, because their only aim is pleasure, whatever the object that provides this pleasure. Thumbsucking provides the same pleasure as sucking the breast of the mother; looking at your self provides the same pleasure as looking at another. In *Instincts and their Vicissitudes*, Freud described this indestructibility of the sexual instincts in the following way. (Freud 1915, 127)

(a) Sadism consists in the exercise of violence or power upon some other person as object.
(b) This object is given up and replaced by the subject's self.

The same goes for voyeurism (Freud 1915, 129):

(a) Looking as an activity directed towards an extraneous object.
(b) Giving up of the object and turning of the scopophilic instinct towards a part of the subject's own body.

The loss of the object does not "starve" the sexual instincts; it only makes them narcissistic (i.e. reflexive or autoerotic). Freud's description of the germ cells in *Beyond the Pleasure Principle* (1920) only repeats this indestructibility of the sexual instincts in the language of biology. In 1920, Freud says about the germ cells what he said about the sexual instincts in 1915: "They are peculiarly resistant to external influences." (Freud 1920, 40)

In Freud's description of the infantile trauma in *Inhibitions, Symptoms and Anxiety*, there is no mention of the part played by the sexual instincts, but the sexual instincts greatly complicate Freud's analysis of infantile trauma. The sexual instincts are always active, even when the child is in a situation of radical passivity. The absence of the mother puts the infant in a position of complete helplessness, but the sexual instincts do not share this fate. The absence of the mother only makes the sexual instincts *reflexive, not passive*.

Because of this peculiarity of the sexual instincts, the reaction to the trauma must be described on two different levels. On the one hand, the trauma produces a situation of radical passivity that will later be repeated compulsively. On the other hand, the trauma produces narcissism, because after the loss of the object the sexual instincts become reflexive or autoerotic. This double reaction to the trauma, utter helplessness and narcissism, also shows us why Freud transformed the ego-instincts into the death instinct and the sexual instincts into Eros. The ego-instincts make the infant extremely vulnerable; the sexual instincts are indestructible and defend it against trauma by becoming reflexive.

Conclusion

Freud's speculations about the death instinct only make sense when we relate them to his analysis of traumatic neurosis, so that the death instinct shows itself as the compulsion to repeat traumatic experiences. These traumas revive an original trauma, i.e. the situation of complete helplessness of the infant in the absence of its mother. A narrow escape from death at the front can only be traumatic because it revives the loss of the primal object, which made the infant helpless towards the ego-instincts that attack it from within. This original trauma, however, also has an effect upon the sexual instincts: it makes them narcissistic.

Note, however, that Freud traced traumatic neurosis back to an infantile trauma. Because of this reference to a *universal* infantile experience, the compulsion to repeat and the narcissistic state of the sexual instincts become universal characteristics of the human condition, not just symptoms of traumatic neurosis. To highlight this point, we could contrast Freud's position with the position of other analysts, such as Winnicott, for whom the death instinct is not crucially important. According to Winnicott, "there are very roughly speaking two kinds of human being, those who do not carry with them a significant experience of mental breakdown in earliest infancy and those who do carry around with them such an experience and who must therefore flee from it, flirt with it, fear it, and to some extent be always preoccupied with the threat of it." (Winnicott 1989, 122) According to Freud, on the other hand, there is only one kind of human being. We all went through the archaic danger-situations related to the loss of the primal object.[23] These infantile traumas must even be considered as the origin of the traumatic kernel of the unconscious.[24]

---

[23] In other texts, Winnicott, too, seems to consider these "primitive agonies" as "universal phenomena". (Winnicott 1989, 88)

[24] In *Inhibitions, Symptoms and Anxiety* (1926), Freud says, "It is highly probable that the immediate precipitating causes of primal repressions are quantitative factors such as an excessive force of excitation and the breaking through of the protective shield against stimuli." (Freud 1926, 94)

All the passions of the human heart are attempts to "suffer" this traumatic kernel, to "flee from it, flirt with it, fear it and to some extent be always preoccupied with the threat of it". Because of the traumatic kernel of the unconscious, the subject is essentially concerned with its own disappearance, and subjectivity *is* this continual, compulsive repetition of and resistance to its own disappearance in a radical passivity (Bernet 2000, 141). Thus, we do not need the reference to a Freudian biology to explain why we are all "held down by the yoke of compulsion that enslaves us." (Sophocles 1996, 299)

7. Oedipus: Abandonment and Exile

Like Oedipus, we were all abandoned by the ones who cared for us. We all experienced the nameless dread produced by the absence of the mother.[1] But that was not the end of the story; it is only the beginning. More and more, Freud will stress the importance of the Oedipal phantasies, which enable the subject to *interpret* the loss of the primal object *retrospectively*.

In *The Infantile Genital Organisation* (1923), Freud introduces the phallic stage. This addition to his theory of infantile sexuality must be understood in relation to the introduction of the death instinct in 1920, because the idea of the death instinct transforms the function of sexuality in Freud's theory. After 1920, Freud's sexual theory lays more and more stress on the castration complex. In this chapter, we will show how this is connected to the introduction of the death instinct.

The phallic-Oedipal organisation

According to Freud, two kinds of infantile danger-situations must be distinguished. On the one hand there is the danger connected to the absence of the mother. This danger is conditioned by the biological helplessness and dependence of the infant. The need to be loved, which persists throughout life, is a consequence of this biological helplessness.[2] However, another danger must also be distinguished. Freud says, "It is a curious thing that early contact with *the demands of sexuality* should have a similar effect on the ego to that produced by premature contact with the external world." (Freud 1926, 155, my emphasis) As in the case of birth or hunger, sexual excitation produces a tension that cannot be mastered by the child.[3] According to Freud, then, the child

---

[1] *Cf.* Bion: "The infant who started with a fear he was dying ends up by containing a nameless dread." (Bion 1962, 96)

[2] "The biological factor, then, establishes the earliest situations of danger and creates the need to be loved which will accompany the child through the rest of its life." (Freud 1926, 155) Here, Freud traces the love of the child for his parents back to its dependence upon them. The child loves them because it needs them. In the *Three Essays* (1905) and in *Instincts and their Vicissitudes* (1915), on the other hand, Freud emphasised the *sexual* origin of love. This change of view concerning the origin of love is maybe the most fundamental consequence of the introduction of the death instinct. From now on, Freud considers love as a consequence of the infant's radical dependence, not as derived from the search for pleasure.

[3] "In early infancy the individual is really not equipped to master psychically the large sums of excitation that reach him whether from without or from within." (Freud 1926, 146)

is "traumatised" twice: once by its vital needs, and once by its sexual needs.

However, these two dangers must be clearly distinguished, because the ego reacts to them in a different way. In the absence of the mother, the infant is confronted with vital needs it cannot satisfy by itself. The hungry child will hallucinate the image of the mother or the mother's breast. This image of the mother is based on the *memory* of the mother actually feeding the child.[4] After a while, however, the child starts to panic, because without its mother it is overpowered by the tension produced by its ego-instincts. Now, the child experiences complete helplessness.

A few years later, the child is confronted with a new experience: *genital excitation*. This time, however, there is nothing to hallucinate. The child has no memory traces to cathect because, unlike oral or anal excitation, genital excitation is not connected to the satisfaction of a vital need. The child has no memories of sexual intercourse.[5] Therefore, the child's own genital excitation appears as an *enigma*.[6] I do not think that there is clinical evidence that the child would be traumatised by this early genital excitation. Genital excitation is puzzling, not traumatic. It demands research into sexual matters and awakens sexual curiosity.[7]

In *The Infantile Genital Organization* (1923), Freud introduces the phallic stage. At a certain moment the child becomes preoccupied with the sensations in his penis: "This part of the body, which is easily excitable, prone to changes and so rich in sensations, occupies the boy's interest to a high degree and is constantly setting new tasks to his instinct for research." (1923, 142) Thus, genital excitation heightens the boy's sexual curiosity, because now he starts to wonder about the function of the phallus.[8]

---

[4] "The child's mnemic image of the person longed for is no doubt intensely cathected, probably in a hallucinatory way at first." (Freud 1926, 137)

[5] "The child may have had only very vague notions as to what constitutes a satisfying erotic intercourse." (Freud 1924, 176)

[6] I agree with Laplanche that sexuality is enigmatic for the child, but in my interpretation, which remains closer to Freud's, this enigma comes primarily from the child's own body, not from the adult. What is enigmatic is the child's own *genital* excitation, because he has no memory of genital intercourse. For a presentation of Laplanche's position, see: Laplanche 1994, 125

[7] "The driving force which this male portion of the body will develop later at puberty expresses itself at this period of life mainly as an urge to investigate, as sexual curiosity." (Freud 1923, 143)

[8] "He wants to see it in other people as well, so as to compare it with his own; and he behaves as though he had a vague idea that this organ could and should be bigger.... Many of the acts of exhibitionism and aggression which children commit, and which in later years would be judged without hesitation to be expressions of lust, prove in analysis to be experiments undertaken in the service of sexual research." (Freud 1923, 143) This seems to imply that the child's sexual phantasies are primarily motivated by the search for knowledge rather that by the search for pleasure.

At the same time, however, the boy's genital excitation "troubles" the relation with his parents. Up until now, he has had a tender relation to his parents. He needed their love and he depended on them for his survival.[9] In the phallic stage, however, a connection is established in the boy's mind between his interest in his penis and his relation to his parents.[10] How does this connection come about? Of course, the mother becomes the object of the child's sexual desire; she cared for his needs before; she will take care of this one too. In the case of little Hans, for instance, it was clear how his interest in widdlers became related to his wish to "coax" with his mother. (Freud 1909, 23) Freud says that, for Hans, "to coax" means "to caress" (Freud 1909, 23), but the idiosyncratic expression "to coax *with* someone" shows that the boy is trying to understand what constitutes sexual intercourse: "Certainly the penis must play a part in it, for the sensations in his own organ were evidence of that." (Freud 1924, 176)

The child also discovers, therefore, that his father, whose widdler must be much bigger than his own, must have something to do with things.[11] This discovery introduces the boy into the Oedipal situation: "His identification with his father then takes on a hostile colouring and changes into a wish to get rid of his father in order to take his place with his mother." (Freud 1923, 32) In *The Infantile Genital Organization*, Freud emphasised the fact that the boy is introduced into a new sphere of sexual curiosity and phantasy *because* he has to make sense of his own genital excitation. In this way, the boy discovers the sexual role of the father. At the same time, this role of the father remains obscure to the child. He only understands that the father must have something to do with it and that the penis must have something to do with it.

In the analysis of little Hans in 1908, Freud only analysed the *positive* Oedipus complex. Freud expressed this idea of a positive Oedipus complex for the first time in a letter to Fliess of October 15, 1897: "I have found, in my own case too, [the phenomenon of] being in love with my mother and jealous of my father, and I now consider it a universal event in early childhood." (Freud 1985, 272) He also mentioned it in *The Interpretation of Dreams*

---

[9] "As regards the prehistory of the Oedipus complex in boys we are far from complete clarity. We know that that period includes an identification of an affectionate sort with the boy's father, an identification which is still free from any sense of rivalry in regard to his mother." (Freud 1925, 250)

[10] "With this new sexual intensity come different mental representations as the child imagines the mother's and the father's body in more distinctly sexual terms. The mind is more fully occupied by sexuality." (Bollas 2000, 13)

[11] "His father not only knew where children came from, he actually performed it—the thing that Hans could only obscurely divine. The widdler must have something to do with it, for his own grew excited whenever he thought of these things—and it must be a big widdler too, bigger than Hans's own." (Freud 1909, 134)

(1900) in the chapter on typical dreams.[12] Also in his analyses of Dora (1905), of Little Hans (1908), and of the Ratman (1909), he focuses on the positive Oedipus complex.

Freud encounters the *negative* Oedipus complex for the first time in the analysis of the Wolfman (1918).[13] The Wolfman was seduced by his sister when he was three years old: "His sister had taken hold of his penis and played with it." (Freud 1918, 20) He remains fixated to the passive sexual aim, but not to his sister: "He pursued a path from his sister via his Nanya to his father." (Freud 1918, 27) Apparently, the transition from a heterosexual to a homosexual object-choice did not constitute a problem in this period of his childhood: "It was a matter of indifference to him whether he reached this aim with a man or with a woman." (Freud 1918, 46) From that moment on, the father becomes the object of the boy's passion.

In 1918, however, Freud does not consider this negative or inverted Oedipus complex a universal phenomenon.[14] It is only in *The Ego and the Id* (1923) that he will present the complete Oedipus complex, both positive and inverted, as universal: "A boy has not merely an ambivalent attitude towards his father and an affectionate object-choice towards his mother, but at the same time he also behaves like a girl and displays an affectionate feminine attitude to his father and a corresponding jealousy and hostility towards his mother." (Freud 1923, 33) The universal occurrence of this positive and negative Oedipus complex is due to "the constitutional bisexuality of each individual." (Freud 1923, 31)

It might be asked, however, if there is clinical evidence for the universality of *all* the aspects of the complete Oedipus complex. Especially the rivalry with the mother in the boy's negative Oedipus complex does not seem to be a universal, clinical fact. Freud seems to share this doubt. In *The Dissolution of the Oedipus Complex* (1924), he says that in the boy's negative Oedipus complex, the boy loves his father and, therefore, the mother becomes *superfluous*, not a rival.[15]

---

[12] "It is the fate of all of us, perhaps, to direct our first sexual impulse towards our mother and our first hatred and our first murderous wish against our father. Our dreams convince us that that is so. King Oedipus, who slew his father Laïus and married his mother Jocasta, merely shows us the fulfilment of our own childhood wishes." (Freud 1900, 262)
[13] *From the History of an Infantile Neurosis* (1918).
[14] "Let us, however, plainly understand that the sexual development of the case that we are now examining has a great disadvantage from the point of view of research, for it was by no means undisturbed." (Freud 1918, 47)
[15] "He could put himself in his father's place in a masculine fashion and have intercourse with his mother as his father did, in which case he would soon have felt the latter as a *hindrance*; or he might want to take the place of his mother and be loved by his father, in which case his mother would become *superfluous*." (Freud 1924, 176, my emphasis)

It is remarkable that the Oedipus complex is not mentioned in the theoretical works on sexuality before 1923, while it already had a central role in the early case-studies. In the first editions of the *Three Essays* (1905, 1910, 1915) and in the papers on *Metapsychology* (1915), there is no reference to it. Laplanche and Pontalis have pointed out that Freud was unable to explain the relation between infantile sexuality, phantasy, and the Oedipus complex. If infantile sexuality is an endogenous, spontaneous, and organic process, sexual phantasies become obsolete. In the theory of seduction, phantasies had an important function; they had to disguise and ennoble the memories of the real seduction. When infantile sexuality becomes an endogenous process, sexual phantasy and the Oedipus complex become a purely imaginary efflorescence, superadded to this endogenous, organic process (Laplanche & Pontalis 1985, 45).

This is the major problem of *Totem and Taboo* (1912), in which Freud presents the positive Oedipus complex as a phylogenetic heritage. Following a hint from Darwin, Freud presents the idea that the original pre-human communities were dominated by a tyrannical patriarch who possessed all the females. This excluded the sons from sexual intercourse. History began when the sons killed the father and ate him. Once their hatred was satisfied, however, the other side of the ambivalent relation to the father made itself felt. The sons not only hated their father; they also loved and admired him, and after the murder, this love produced a feeling of guilt and a retrospective obedience to the dead father. The dead father appeared more powerful than the living one, and the sons denied themselves the very sexual intercourse with the women of the clan that they had killed the father to gain. Thus was the incest taboo established. (Freud 1913, 143)

According to Freud, we see this phylogenetic heritage repeated in the life of every child. This hypothesis of ontogenesis as a repetition of phylogenesis is problematic enough even in its own terms. Furthermore, however, it does not solve the question of the relation between the Oedipus complex and the *auto-erotism* of infantile sexuality. The relation between the Oedipus complex and the child's curiosity about the function of the father remains equally unintelligible. Before the introduction of the phallic stage in 1923, Freud could not elaborate the relation between his three most important hypotheses: infantile sexuality, the infantile sexual theories, and the Oedipus complex.

The Oedipus Complex in Three Primal Phantasies

In 1923, Freud introduced the phallic stage, and this enabled him to present a comprehensive picture of the child's sexual life. As we will see, Freud's article on *The Infantile Genital Organization* (1923) is not just an addition to his sexual theory as presented in the *Three Essays* (1905); rather, Freud's works of the 1920s contain a completely new elaboration of his sexual theory and his psychopathology.

We have seen above how the child is introduced into the Oedipus situation because he is confronted with his own genital excitation. Genital excitation is enigmatic because, unlike oral or anal excitation, it is not connected to the satisfaction of a vital need. Therefore, genital excitation becomes the source of sexual curiosity. The child will now patch together sexual phantasies from things he has seen, heard, and experienced in the past. Freud gives the example of a child listening to his parents copulating. In the phallic stage, the child retrospectively understands the meaning of what he heard previously. (Freud 1925, 250) This "understanding" must not be interpreted too intellectually. It means that in the phallic stage, the child connects the sexual intercourse of the parents to his own genital excitation because listening to the parents copulating now arouses him. This retrospective understanding results in three stereotypical phantasies: seduction, the primal scene (parents copulating), and castration.

In the phallic stage, the caresses of the mother begin to arouse genital excitation, and the affectionate relation to the mother thus becomes sexualised. This produces the phantasy of the mother as the seducer who is at the origin of my sexuality. This phantasy of an adult who implanted sexuality in the child initially misled Freud, and he believed his patients when they complained that they had been introduced to sexuality by an adult when they were children. It was the confusion between this phantasy and reality that lay at the root of Freud's seduction theory.

In his study of the Wolfman (1918) and in his *Introductory Lectures* (1917), however, Freud conceives of seduction as a primal phantasy. This does not mean that he thought that real seduction never happened. Freud certainly believed that the Wolfman was seduced by his sister.[16] But this seduction could only *affect* him in the phallic stage, when he was capable of genital excitation. As it so happened, the Wolfman's sister played with his penis when he was three years old, but even had she done so when he was one year old, it would not have affected him until he was three, because only then would he have been able to interpret its meaning retrospectively. The production of phantasies thus follows a biologic: sexual phantasies about earlier events are produced in the phallic stage and in puberty, and as we have seen above, the same goes for the primal scene. The Wolfman saw his parents making love when he was one and a half years old, but he only understood its meaning (in a dream) when he was four years old.

Freud sees the same retrospective understanding at work in the primal phantasy of castration. In the analysis of little Hans, Freud emphasised that the threat of castration, as such, did not scare Hans one bit (Freud 1909, 8), and neither was he frightened by the sight of the female genitals as such.[17] It is

---

[16] "With my patient, his seduction by his elder sister was an indisputable reality; why should not the same have been true of his observation of his parents' intercourse?" (Freud 1918, 97)

[17] "They disavow the fact and believe that they *do* see a penis, all the same." (Freud 1923, 143)

only in the phallic stage that the child starts to wonder about the function of his penis, and only then can the discovery that some people do not have a penis become emotionally significant. In *The Infantile Genital Organization* (1923), Freud stresses that "the significance of the castration complex can only be rightly appreciated if its origin in the phase of phallic primacy is also taken into account." (Freud 1923, 144)

The boy's research into sexual matters confronts him with the problem of sexual difference; and it is in the context of this research that the sight of the female genitals and the threat of castration become significant. The combination of these two experiences (threat and spectacle) enables the boy to solve the question of sexual difference. The boy now interprets the lack of a penis as a punishment: "The lack of a penis is the result of having been castrated as a punishment." (Freud 1923, 144) Girls are bad boys who were punished. This phallic interpretation of sexual difference explains the depreciation and horror of women in "grown-up boys", and it also explains the deferred obedience to the threat of castration. What already happened to them can also happen to me.

These three primal phantasies, then, are the results of the child's sexual awakening. They are answers to three interconnected questions. The phantasy of seduction is an interpretation of the origin or the cause of the child's genital excitation. The phantasy of the primal scene is an interpretation of the sexuality of the parents. Castration is an interpretation of sexual difference. At the same time, these three phantasies cover the different dimensions of the Oedipal situation. They sexualise the boy's tender relation with his mother and, in the inverted Oedipus complex, with his father (seduction) and the relation between the mother and the father (primal scene). The phantasy of castration not only explains sexual difference; it also produces the terrifying figure of the father that excludes the boy from sexual intercourse with the mother and, in the inverted Oedipus complex, with the father himself.

The phantasy of castration is the apogee and the end of sexual curiosity. The interpretation of sexual difference in terms of castration produces the fear that I, too, will be castrated by the father. In *Inhibitions, Symptoms and Anxiety* (1926), Freud takes up the analyses of little Hans and the Wolfman again, and stresses the fact that the two boys took up different positions in the Oedipal situation. In the case of little Hans, Freud only analysed the positive Oedipus complex; Hans's relation with his mother is sexualised, and this produces hostility towards his father. At the same time, Hans maintains an affectionate relation to his father, and his relation to his father therefore becomes ambivalent. Because of his hostility towards his father, Hans fears his father's retaliation.[18] The father

---

18 "Let us imagine that he is a young servant who is in love with the mistress of the house and has received some tokens of her favour. He hates his master, who is more powerful than he is, and he would like to have him out of the way. It would than be eminently natural for him to dread his master's vengeance and to develop a fear of him." (Freud 1926, 102)

will castrate him because of his interest in his "widdler" and the sexualisation of his relation to his mother, and thus the fear of castration leads to a repression of the Oedipus complex.[19]

In the case of the Wolfman, the analysis revealed the dominance of an inverted Oedipus complex. The boy had "a passive, tender impulse to be loved by him [his father] in a genital-erotic sense." (Freud 1926, 105) However, the phantasy of castration, as an interpretation of sexual difference, leads to a repression of this impulse because "a relation of that sort presupposed a sacrifice of his genitals—of the organ which distinguished him from a female." (Freud 1926, 108) Here, it is not the hostility towards the father that is blocked by the fear of castration, but the feminine attitude towards him. Thus, in both cases, the phantasy of castration leads to a repression of the Oedipal wish-impulses.

In *Totem and Taboo*, Freud gave a phylogenetic explanation for the Oedipus complex. However, our analysis of how the Oedipal phantasies can be understood as answers to the enigmas of genital sexuality shows that the Oedipus complex does not need an explanation in terms of phylogenesis.[20] At a certain moment, strange things start to happen in the boy's penis. This awakens his curiosity about his penis; the caresses of the mother become seductions; and the boy wants to compare his penis with the penises of his mother and his father. His research into these matters produces primal phantasies. The phantasy of castration, which should solve the problem of sexual difference, frightens the boy and motivates the repression of his sexual phantasies. Now, he becomes stupid; he is ready for primary school.[21]

Castration as a Modification of Earlier Traumas

In his works of the twenties, Freud considers castration as the crucial element in all psychopathologies: in neurosis, perversion and psychosis.[22] Is it possible that the whole of psychopathology is caused by a fear of something that never

---

[19] "The process of repression had attacked almost all the components of his Oedipus complex—both his hostile and his tender impulses towards his father and his tender impulses towards his mother." (Freud 1926, 106)

[20] In 1913, Freud gave a phylogenetic explanation of the Oedipus complex (See above). It is only in his later work that he explained the function of the Oedipus complex on an ontogenetic level.

[21] In *The Question of Lay Analysis* (1926), Freud says, "I have an impression that with the onset of the latency period they become mentally inhibited as well, stupider. From that time on, too, many lose their physical charm." (Freud 1926, 215)

[22] In a letter of September 1926 to Edoardo Weiss, Freud says, "I could not name any neurosis in which this complex is not to be met with."(Freud 1914, 93) In *A Child Is Being Beaten* (1919) and in *Outline* (1940), Freud shows that the same goes for perversion and psychosis.

happens? Freud himself asked this question in *Inhibitions, Symptoms and Anxiety*: "Is it absolutely certain that fear of castration is the only motive force of repression (or defence)?" (Freud 1926, 123)

In the previous chapter, we already discussed the earlier anxiety-situations of the infant, which were connected to the loss of the primal object. The fear of castration is only the last link in a concatenation of infantile anxieties, and these subsequent anxiety-situations (birth, loss of the object, castration) reinforce one another.[23] This succession of dangers, right from birth, through the loss of the object, to castration, is at the same time a modification of anxiety. A transition takes place from traumatic situations to danger-situations, or from automatic anxiety to anxiety as a signal of danger. How does this come about?

Birth and hunger are experienced by the infant as purely economic disturbances. After a while, the infant learns that the absence of the mother will provoke hunger, and therefore starts to consider the absence of the mother *per se* as a danger, even if its needs are satisfied at the moment. In this way, the infant is able to anticipate the danger, and anxiety becomes a *signal* of danger: "The situation of missing its mother is not a danger-situation but a traumatic one. Or, to put it more correctly, it is a traumatic situation if the infant happens at the time to be feeling a need which its mother should be the one to satisfy. It turns into a danger-situation if this need is not present at the moment." (Freud 1926, 170) The infant now fears the absence of the mother as such because it *anticipates* the situation of hunger and utter helplessness. Anticipation distinguishes a danger-situation from a traumatic one. (Freud 1926, 166)

How does castration fit into this process of modification of anxiety? The fear of castration is a very peculiar anxiety because castration never happens. Freud does not emphasise this peculiarity of castration, although it seems crucial to his argument.[24] In castration anxiety, the danger is *only* in the anticipation. The anxiety is a *pure signal* of danger, and thus castration anxiety can become the most radical modification of the earlier, traumatic situations. How does this modification of anxiety come about?

Castration, like the earlier anxiety-situations, signifies a loss of the primal object: "Ferenczi has traced, quite correctly, I think, a clear line of connection between this fear [of castration] and the fears contained in the earlier situations of danger." (Freud 1926, 139) The possession of the penis guarantees the possibility of a return to the mother in copulation. Therefore, castration implies a renewed separation from the mother. But castration is the *phallic interpretation* of the loss of the primal object, in which the loss of the primal object is

---

[23] "All these danger-situations and determinants of anxiety can persist side by side and cause the ego to react to them with anxiety at a period later than the appropriate one; or, again, several of them can come into operation at the same time." (Freud 1926, 142)

[24] Otto Rank, on the other hand, laid great stress upon the *Unernst* of castration. (Rank 1924, 24)

sexualised and attributed to the father. The boy has to abandon the sexual relation with the mother because otherwise the father will castrate him. In this way, the phantasy of castration is a new way of experiencing the traumatic loss of the mother.

This time, however, that loss is no longer traumatic, because castration is always anticipated and it never happens.[25] The phantasy of castration transforms the compulsion to repeat the trauma into an endless anticipation of danger. It is also a sexualisation of this danger because, in the phantasy of castration, *the loss of the mother* is transformed into *a prohibition of sexual intercourse with the mother*. The Oedipus and castration complexes, which originated from the boy's curiosity about his own sexuality, produce a sexualisation of his infantile traumas, and therefore an anticipation of the catastrophe that already happened.

Conclusion

Our interpretation of the death instinct and the phallic-Oedipal organisation contains all the elements of the story of Oedipus. The Oedipus complex is not restricted any longer to the murder of the father and incest with the mother. It also refers to the fact that Oedipus was abandoned by his parents (the original trauma), to the Sphinx as an enigmatic figure (the enigmas of adult sexuality), to Oedipus's curiosity and his demand to know the truth (the boy's curiosity), as well as to his punishment (phantasy of castration), which turns out to be a repetition of the abandonment he experienced as an infant. The pierced eyes of the blind exile reflect the pierced feet of the abandoned child.

---

[25] "The individual will have made an important advance in his capacity for self-preservation if he can foresee and expect a traumatic situation of this kind which entails helplessness, instead of simply waiting for it to happen." (Freud 1926, 166)

8. The Minoan-Mycenaean Civilisation

After 1920, Freud centred his sexual theory on the Oedipus and castration complexes. This highlighted the problem of female sexuality, because the Oedipus complex cannot have the same outcome with the girl. According to Freud, the castration complex introduces the girl into the Oedipal situation, while it is the end of the Oedipus complex in the boy. Furthermore, the phantasy of castration does not produce anxiety in the girl; castration has already happened, and instead becomes the source of penis envy and disappointment.

The fact that castration is the beginning of the Oedipus complex in girls leads Freud to the discovery of the pre-Oedipal phase. Penis envy and the girl's hostility towards the mother cannot be understood as effects of the castration complex alone. They are phallic modifications of "the general dissatisfaction of children." (Freud 1931, 234) Together with traumatic neurosis, female sexuality points to a psychic realm that is not dominated by castration anxiety. The introduction of the pre-oedipal phase in Freud's works on female sexuality will allow us to further elaborate our interpretation of the relation between the castration complex and the death instinct.

Female Sexuality versus Infantile Sexuality (1905)

Freud's ideas on female sexuality have been criticised ever since they were first published, and still are today. Female psychoanalysts and feminists have argued that Freud presented a crude, male phantasy of female sexuality. True though this may be, Freud's critics seem to ignore the fact that Freud's view of human nature, and especially of human sexuality, is derived from the analysis of pathological symptoms. In the *Three Essays*, Freud says, "Clinical observation of these abnormalities will have drawn our attention to *amalgamations* which have been lost to view in the uniform behaviour of normal people." (Freud 1905, 162) In the case of female sexuality, this implies that Freud addressed the problem through the analysis of the pathologies of his female patients, and therefore that his view of female sexuality is based on the analysis of hysteria, female homosexuality, paranoia and masochism, just as his view of male sexuality resulted from the analysis of fetishism, voyeurism, male homosexuality and psychic impotence. In Freud's view, only the analysis of neurosis and perversion can reveal the structure of human sexuality.

In the third of the *Three Essays*, "The Transformations of Puberty", Freud discusses sexual differentiation between men and women. According to Freud, this differentiation happens in puberty. This implies that there is only one kind of infantile sexuality: "The auto-erotic activity of the erotogenic zones is, however, the same in both sexes, and owing to this uniformity there is no possibility of a distinction between the two sexes such as arises after puberty." (Freud 1905, 219) At the same time, Freud says that infantile sexuality, even the infantile sexuality of girls, is "of a wholly masculine character." (1905, 219) Of course, it is only in retrospect that infantile sexuality can be characterised as masculine. In boys, puberty produces an increase in sexual desire, which also re-awakens their infantile sexual tendencies.[1] In so far as boys are able to give in to these infantile tendencies by sublimating them[2] or by integrating them into their sexual life, infantile sexuality can retrospectively be considered as masculine because, in fact, male sexuality remains marked by infantile sexuality.

Female sexuality, on the other hand, is characterised by the *repression* of infantile sexuality. According to Freud, "Puberty, which brings about so great an accession of libido in boys, is marked in girls by a fresh wave of *repression*." (Freud 1905, 220) Unlike male sexuality, female sexuality cannot be considered as a re-awakening of infantile sexuality, because unlike the penis, the vagina was not an erotogenic zone in childhood. When little Hans enters puberty, he has only to pick up his old interest in his widdler again.[3] The closest little girls get to genital sexuality, however, is clitoridal sexuality. Therefore, female sexuality is a specifically adult sexuality because the vagina is a *new* erotogenic zone.[4]

As such, however, this idea of a transference of excitability from the clitoris to the vagina in the development of female sexuality is not very convincing. Only the neurotic symptoms of vaginismus and sexual anaesthesia make this idea intelligible. For most girls, the first sexual intercourse is not particularly enjoyable. Some girls experience it without any pleasure (anaesthesia) and some girls are unable to have intercourse at all (vaginismus). This does not imply that they have an aversion for every sexual pleasure; on the contrary, "they are anaesthetic at the vaginal orifice but are by no means incapable of excitement originating in the clitoris or even in other zones." (Freud 1905, 221) These girls hold on to their infantile sources of pleasure, while genital intercourse does not become a new source of pleasure.

---

[1] "The sexual life of maturing youth is almost entirely restricted to indulging in phantasies, that is, in ideas that are not destined to be carried into effect. In these phantasies the infantile tendencies invariably emerge once more, but this time with intensified pressure from somatic sources." (Freud 1905, 226)

[2] Inventing sexual jokes, for instance.

[3] "When erotogenic susceptibility to stimulation has been succesfully transferred by a woman from the clitoris to the vaginal orifice, it implies that she had adopted a *new* leading zone for the purposes of her later sexual activity. A man, on the other hand, retains his leading zone unchanged from childhood." (Freud 1905, 221, my emphasis)

[4] "Thus in female development there is a process of transition from the one phase to the other, to which *there is nothing analogous in the male*." (Freud 1931, 228, my emphasis)

These clinical phenomena reveal that in female sexuality the conflict between genital and infantile sexuality is more pronounced than in male sexuality. This is why Freud can say that female sexuality is based on the repression of infantile sexuality: "The fact that women change their leading erotogenic zone in this way, together with the wave of repression at puberty, which, as it were, puts aside their childish masculinity, are the chief determinants of the greater proneness of women to neurosis and especially to hysteria." (Freud 1905, 221) The conflict between infantile and adult sexuality, which is more pronounced in girls, is also at the origin of neurosis. That is why there is more neurosis than perversion in women.

Freud then adds this very important and, at first sight, insulting remark: "These determinants, therefore, are intimately related to *the essence of femininity*." (Freud 1905, 221, my emphasis) In this quote, Freud relates vaginismus, sexual anaesthesia, and hysteria to the essence of femininity. But then what does Freud mean by "the essence of femininity" if he only understands it from the perspective of pathology? According to Freud, neurosis is the privilege of human beings. (Freud 1926, 211) Human beings are the only mammals that can become neurotic or perverse, and there must therefore exist some biological condition that makes it so. For Freud, this biological condition could only be the two-phased onset of sexuality in infancy and puberty.

This double onset of sexuality is indeed a biological fact that is specific to the human animal. It is also one of the determinants of our privelege to become neurotic.[5] In puberty, a conflict breaks out between the recathexis of infantile sources of pleasure and their primal repression. Neurosis and perversion are the two solutions to this conflict, and normal sexuality is only an amalgamation of both. In women, this conflict between infantile sexuality and its repression is intensified by the discovery of the vagina as a new erotogenic zone. Women will tend towards neurosis rather than perversion because vaginal sexuality implies a *new* repression of infantile sexuality. For women, therefore, the infantile, clitoridal sexuality "becomes" their childish masculinity.

The idea of neurosis as a human privilege is one of the fundamental ideas of psychoanalysis. From this perspective, the link between hysteria and femininity cannot be understood as an insult to women. Female sexuality *per se* is not a privilege of human females, but its pathologies are, because they are determined by the specifically human two-phased onset of sexuality—by the conflict between infantile and adult sexuality. Therefore, to think what is specifically human about female sexuality, we must first of all understand its pathological forms. As we saw above, Freud said in the *Three Essays* that sexual anaesthesia and hysteria are intimately related, not to female sexuality, but

---

[5] "This 'diphasic onset', as it is named, of sexual life has a great deal to do with the genesis of neurotic illnesses. It seems to occur only in human beings, and it is perhaps one of the determinants of the human privilege of becoming neurotic." (Freud 1926, 211)

to the essence of femininity (Freud 1905, 221), and this highlights the fact that, for Freud, sexual psychopathology reveals what is specifically human about human sexuality. Just as fetishism and voyeurism elucidated the peculiar aesthetic conditions of the sexual object-choice of human beings in general, so do the pathologies of female sexuality reveal femininity, as that which is specifically human in that sexuality.

The Girl's Castration-Complex (1925)

To understand female sexuality in its anthropological dimension and not just biologically, it is necessary to take female psychopathology into account. What are the conditions required for paranoia, homosexuality, masochism and hysteria to develop in women? In the *Three Essays*, Freud gave a first answer to this question by pointing to the specifically human two-phased onset of sexuality. In his later works, he will further develop his ideas about female sexuality.

As we have seen in the previous chapter, the introduction of the phallic stage, and thus of an infantile *genital* organisation, greatly complicates Freud's initial theory of sexuality. In the *Three Essays*, he emphasised the uniformity of infantile sexuality in boys and girls. With the introduction of the phallic stage, this uniformity of infantile sexuality cannot be maintained. In the 1920s, the centre of Freud's theory of sexuality shifts to the Oedipus and castration complexes. In the phallic stage, the boy establishes a positive and an inverted Oedipus complex, and the fear of castration becomes the motive for the repression of those complexes.[6] With girls, on the other hand, there can naturally be no fear of castration.[7] Between 1915 and 1920, Freud published three important papers on specific pathologies in women: *A Case of Paranoia Running Counter to the Psychoanalytic Theory of the Disease* (1915), *A Child is Being Beaten* (1919), and *The Psychogenesis of a Case of Female Homosexuality* (1920). However, it is only in 1925 that he starts to develop a theory of female sexuality that can account for these pathologies from the perspective of the infantile genital organisation.

In 1925, Freud writes *Some Psychical Consequences of the Anatomical Distinction Between the Sexes*. In this work, he analyses the castration complex in women. Unlike the boy, whose first reaction to the sight of the female genitals is one of disavowal, the girl immediately understands: she has seen the penis "and knows that she is without it and wants to have it." (Freud 1925, 252) Freud here contradicts his former idea that infantile sexuality is masculine.

---

[6] See the previous chapter.
[7] "Is it absolutely certain that the fear of castration is the only motive force of repression (or defence)? If we think of neuroses in women we are bound to doubt it." (Freud 1926, 123)

Already in childhood, the girl is confronted with the problem of sexual difference in a different way than the boy.

In the *Three Essays*, Freud had emphasised the radical distinction between infantile, autoerotic sexuality and adult, genital sexuality. The introduction of the infantile genital organisation in 1923 relativised this distinction.[8] The child is capable of sexual object-choice and of genital excitation. However, one important difference with adult sexuality remains: "This consists in the fact that, for both sexes, only one genital, namely the male one, comes into account. What is present, therefore, is not the primacy of the genitals, but a primacy of the *phallus*." (Freud 1923, 142) This implies that in the phallic stage, girls start to consider themselves as lacking this phallus and thus as being castrated.[9] This infantile interpretation of the female genitals as "being castrated" is accompanied by a deep feeling of humiliation and disappointment, and this disappointment in lacking the phallus produces a first turning away from clitoridal sexuality.

Apparently, Freud had begun to see that the repression of infantile sexuality in puberty did not give a sufficient explanation of sexual repression. The hypothesis of the castration complex in girls, and of the penis envy that results from it, introduced "a *forerunner* of the wave of repression which at puberty will do away with a large amount of the girl's masculine sexuality in order to make room for the development of her femininity." (Freud 1925, 255, my emphasis) At puberty, vaginal sexuality necessitates a repression of infantile sexuality. According to this later Freud, this repression is itself a repetition of a turning away from sexuality in childhood, and the neurosis of puberty is thus the repetition of an infantile neurosis. In women, this process is complicated by the discovery of the vagina as an erotogenic zone in puberty. Masturbation is therefore more discordant with female sexuality than with male sexuality. Clitoridal masturbation has already turned out disappointing in childhood, and the discovery of the vagina in puberty makes clitoridal masturbation even more incompatible with the specifically adult, vaginal sexuality.

According to Freud, the castration complex in women also explains a specifically feminine ethical position. Freud says that it has been observed throughout the ages that women "show less sense of justice than men, that they are less ready to submit to the great exigencies of life, that they are more often influenced in their judgements by feelings of affection and hostility." (Freud 1925, 258) It is for this kind of remarks, of course, that Freud has been criticised of being a misogynist. Freud's description makes sense, however, in the case of the heroines of Greek tragedy, especially Antigone. She is determined to bury her brother's dead body although Creon, the king, forbids it. She does not care for the good of the state. Only her duty to her brother still

---

[8] *The Infantile Genital Organization* (1923).
[9] "The antithesis here is between having *a male genital* and being *castrated*." (Freud 1923, 145)

matters to her, and she is willing to die for it. But how are this rebellious obstinacy and this lack of anxious anticipation related to the castration complex? Or, why is Antigone's attitude specifically feminine?

In the previous chapter, we have seen that in men castration is something that always remains a threat, something that is always anticipated. A clear example of this is Sophocles's *Oedipus Rex*. The whole play evokes an anticipatory anxiety. During the whole play, the audience *anticipates* the catastrophic moment when Oedipus will discover what he has done. In women, on the other hand, castration has already happened.[10] Sophocles expresses this when he describes Antigone's attitude towards death: "My life has long been dead." (Soph. 1994, 55) The worst has already happened; there is nothing to be afraid of anymore. In this attitude, the girl's castration complex is expressed very clearly. The affect that accompanies it is disappointment, not anxiety. According to Freud, the girl, like the boy, interprets sexual difference in a phallic manner: "He has something that I lack." This phallic interpretation of sexual difference is the infantile root of femininity. It produces a tendency to turn away from sexuality, and a propensity towards obstinacy and rebelliousness. When Freud says that the super-ego of women is weaker than that of men, he seems to envy this feminine lack of castration-anxiety.

The Pre-Oedipal Phase (1931)

In 1931, Freud writes *Female Sexuality*. The pathologies of his female patients had led him to a further exploration of the girl's infantile sexuality. Hysteria and paranoia, he says, reveal the importance of the relation to the mother in a woman's life, and the infantile factor in these pathologies must be sought in the early attachment of the girl to the mother. Before 1931, Freud interpreted the girl's attachment to the father and her hostility towards the mother as an expression of her Oedipus complex. In his paper of 1931, however, he thinks that this idea cannot be maintained as such. He has discovered that the attitude of women towards men is often modelled, not on their relation to their father, but on the early, pre-Oedipal relation to their mother.[11]

This pre-Oedipal fixation was discovered by Ruth Mack-Brunswick, who was Freud's closest collaborator at the time. In her paper, "*Die Analyse eines Eifersuchtswahnes*" (1928), she describes the treatment of a woman who accused her husband of having an affair with her stepmother. (Mack-Brunswick, 1928, 459)

---

[10] "Castration has already had its effect." (Freud 1925, 257). In this way, Oedipus at Colonos resembles Antigone, because the blind Oedipus is also the figure of a castration that already happened.

[11] "The husband of such a woman was meant to be the inheritor of her relation to her father, but in reality he became the inheritor of her relation to her mother." (Freud 1931, 231)

Her own mother had died when she was very young, and she was raised by her older sister, who seduced her into mutual masturbation. (Mack-Brunswick 1928, 464) During the analysis, Brunswick discovers that all the men in this patient's life and in her dreams are actually substitutes for the incestuous sister.

A clear example of this is the nightmare the patient tells during one of the analytic sessions: "A man, who is dressed in black, approaches her and has sex with her. During coitus she is very afraid. She has an orgasm. The man wears a bow tie [*eine Masche*]." (Mack-Brunswick 1928, 462) Brunswick's analysis of this dream showed that the man is a substitute for the sister, and the dream-scene a repetition of the seduction (Mack-Brunswick 1928, 504); the black clothes refer to the burial of the sister, who had died in the meantime, and the sister used to wear a bow tie like the one in the dream. (Mack-Brunswick 1928, 462) Brunswick does not refer to the fact that, in Austrian German, "eine Masche" means not only "a bow tie" but also "a sham". The sister had indeed seduced the patient into mutual masturbation with "eine Masche". (Mack-Brunswick 1928, 462) The analysis of this dream also explained the moment at which the delusion of jealousy occurred; the woman became jealous a few months after her wedding, when sexual intercourse with her husband had re-activated the memory of the seduction by her sister. Having sex with her husband meant being unfaithful to her dead sister.

At first, Brunswick thought the discoveries she made in this analysis were specific to this peculiar case. Later, however, Freud and Brunswick discovered that the essential elements that determined the history of this patient are actually universal moments in the pre-history of us all.[12] According to Brunswick, we do not need an incestuous older sister to be seduced during childhood: "The first attachment to the mother which is so passive in nature, derives its strength and tenacity in great part from her physical care, and of course above all from her feeding of the child. There is no doubt about the sexual nature of the child's response." (Mack-Brunswick 1950, 271) In this way, the physical care of the genitals introduces the girl into masturbation. At first, this masturbation is "unaccompanied by phantasy" (Freud 1931, 233), and only later do the "seductions" by the mother become problematic, because the mother is also the one who *prohibits* masturbation.[13]

---

[12] "I judged this case to be extremely rare, dependent for its existence on the unusual nature and circumstances of the trauma. But the insight gained in this analysis and applied to other patients demonstrated that the difference was merely one of degree, and further that no particular trauma such as seduction is essential for the production of this clinical picture which instead of being exceptional has proved to be extraordinarily common." (Mack-Brunswick 1950, 281)

[13] "Her resentment at being prevented from free sexual activity plays a big part in her detachment from her mother. The same motive comes into operation again after puberty, when her mother takes up her duty of guarding her daughter's chastity." (Freud 1931, 233) With Brunswick's patient, this was also the case. The older sister, who introduced her into masturbation, prohibited it all the same.

The seduction into / prohibition of masturbation by the mother is one of the motives for turning away from her. (1931, 233) The most important motive, however, lies in the castration complex. When the girl discovers that neither she nor her mother possesses a penis, this produces a fatal disappointment.[14] According to Freud, this disappointment with the mother is the most important motive for the turn towards the father. The girl blames her "deficiency" on the mother: "At the end of this first phase of attachment to the mother, there emerges, as the girl's strongest motive for turning away from her, the reproach that her mother did not give her a proper penis—that is to say, brought her into the world as a female." (Freud 1931, 234) But why does the girl transform her disappointment into a grudge against the mother? This cannot be explained by the castration complex as such, and is a question that will lead Freud and Brunswick to the discovery of a "Minoan-Mycenaean civilisation behind the civilisation of Greece." (Freud 1931, 226)

The girl's reproach against her mother has its roots in the earliest experiences of the infant in the relation with the mother. When the girl reproaches her mother for not *giving* her a penis, then this reproach is a phallic translation of the more archaic reproach that she did not give her enough milk and did not suckle her long enough.[15] The phallic reproach is a modification of a more archaic hostility. This early disappointment with the mother, however, is no longer specific to girls: "It would rather seem that this accusation gives expression to the general dissatisfaction of *children*." (Freud 1931, 234, my emphasis) This dissatisfaction is the origin of the hostility towards the mother. This hostility, Freud concludes, is older than the Oedipal rivalry for the love of the father.[16]

In *Female Sexuality* (1931), Freud states explicitly what he already hinted at in *Beyond the Pleasure Principle* (1920) and *Inhibitions, Symptoms and Anxiety* (1926): the castration complex is a modification and a phallic interpretation of a more primordial trauma. We have seen before how, for the boy, the phantasy of castration modifies the loss of the primal object. The phantasy of castration transforms the original trauma into an anticipation of punishment. Therefore, the castration complex is accompanied by fear because fear implies anticipation. In the girl, however, the castration complex is accompanied by

---

[14] "When she comes to understand the general nature of this characteristic, it follows that femaleness—and with it, of course, her mother—suffers a great depreciation in her eyes." (Freud 1931, 233)

[15] "A second reproach, which does not reach quite so far back, is rather a surprising one. It is that her mother did not give her enough milk, did not suckle her long enough." (Freud 1931, 234)

[16] "Their hostile attitude to their mother is not a consequence of the rivalry implicit in the Oedipus complex, but originates from the preceding phase and has merely been reinforced and exploited in the Oedipus situation." (Freud 1931, 231) The same goes for the hostility of the boy towards his mother. The negative Oedipus complex derives its strength from the pre-Oedipal phase.

the affects of penis envy and disappointment. These affects too are a phallic modification of a more primordial disappointment in the early relation with the mother. In the case of the girl, however, the castration complex does not provoke anxiety, because for the girl, castration is not a threat; it has already happened.

The pathologies of their female patients thus led Freud and Brunswick to the discovery of the pre-Oedipal phase because in girls the castration complex does not project the primordial trauma in the future as a punishment. Therefore, the castration complex in girls remains closer to the earliest disappointments of infancy. Freud's analysis of female sexuality corroborates our interpretation of the castration complex as a phallic modification of infantile traumas. It is only now, with the introduction of the pre-Oedipal phase, that we can interpret one of Freud's most obscure and "mythological" texts on the death instinct, *The Economic Problem of Masochism* (1924).

Erotogenic Masochism and the Origin of Aggression

In *The Economic Problem of Masochism* (1924), Freud introduces the idea of erotogenic masochism[17] as a sexualisation of the death instinct, and here, he writes about the death instinct without referring to the compulsion to repeat. The death instinct is merely considered as a tendency in every living organism to return to a state of inorganic stability. (Freud 1924, 163) Of course, this could be understood as a tendency to get rid of the restlessness that is essential to life (Freud 1924, 159), but such an interpretation of the death instinct would reduce it to the very general and rather commonplace observation that life is never easy. It is clear that the death instinct cannot be interpreted this way. According to Freud, the death instinct is primarily a tendency towards *self-destruction*,[18] and it is from this perspective that Freud will develop his view of masochism and the origin of aggression.

In *The Economic Problem of Masochism*, Freud explains aggression as a defence against the instinct for *self*-destruction: "The libido has the task of making the destroying instinct innocuous, and it fulfils the task by diverting that instinct to a great extent outwards—soon with the help of a special organic system, the muscular apparatus—towards objects in the external world." (Freud 1924, 163) Aggression towards external objects prevents us

---

[17] He distinguishes erotogenic masochism from moral masochism and feminine or perverse masochism. Erotogenic masochism is, according to Freud, at the origin of the two other forms of masochism. (1924, 161)

[18] "In (multicellular) organisms the libido meets the instinct of death, or destruction, which is dominant in them and which seeks to disintegrate the cellular organism and to conduct each separate unicellular organism into a state of inorganic stability (relative though this may be)." (Freud 1924, 163)

from destroying ourselves. This implies that, for Freud, aggression cannot be understood as a mere reaction to frustration; aggression is first of all a deflection of the instinct for self-destruction.

This deflection into the external world, however, is never a complete one. The instinct for self-destruction can never completely be transformed into aggression towards objects: "Another portion does not share this transposition outwards; it remains inside the organism." (Freud 1924, 163) The only way to deal with this portion of self-destruction, which cannot be transformed into aggression, is to enjoy it. In 1924, Freud does not explain how the organism learns to enjoy its own self-destruction. He refers to the vague notion of "libidinal sympathetic excitation" to explain that pleasure can be a by-product of affects, even painful ones. (Freud 1924, 163) In one way or another, self-destruction is sexualised and becomes "the original, erotogenic masochism." (Freud 1924, 164) This pleasure in self-destruction is extremely dangerous. It anaesthetises the pleasure principle.[19]

As in *Beyond the Pleasure Principle*, Freud's reference to the death instinct in *The Economic Problem of Masochism* does not explain anything. The deflection of the death instinct does not *explain how* aggression originates. The sexualisation of the death instinct does not *explain why* "even the subject's destruction of himself cannot take place without libidinal satisfaction." (1924, 170) In the previous chapter, we interpreted the death instinct as the compulsion to repeat infantile traumas. If this interpretation is correct, it has to allow for an explanation of aggression and erotogenic masochism. It is only after the introduction of the pre-Oedipal phase that we are able to elaborate our interpretation.

It goes without saying that the earliest experiences of the infant are of a passive nature. The infant is born, suckled, cleaned, fed and loved by its mother. The infant's passivity is the effect of its biological helplessness. In the previous chapter, we saw that this helplessness makes the child extremely vulnerable. The absence of the mother leaves the infant alone with the tension produced by its ego-instincts, and this shows that the passivity of the infant is ultimately passivity towards its own instincts.

The *Fort-Da* game revealed how the infant *actively* repeats the loss of the mother, an activity that is based on a fundamental and primitive identification with the mother.[20] The infant does to itself what the mother did to it, and this produces two kinds of activities. On the one hand, the infant actively repeats

---

[19] "If pain and unpleasure can be not simply warnings but actually aims, the pleasure principle is paralysed—it is as though the watchman over our mental life were put out of action by a drug." (Freud 1924, 159)

[20] "It is apparent that the child's earliest activity is, in its outward form at least, a copy of the mother. This is the most fundamental and primitive kind of identification, dependent for its existence solely upon the replacement of passivity by activity and consequently of mother attachment by mother identification, irrespective of any other emotional bond." (Mack-Brunswick, 1950, 267)

the pleasurable experiences it received from the mother (for instance, thumb-sucking). On the other hand, the infant actively repeats the traumatic experiences produced by the loss of the mother (for instance, the *Fort-Da* game).[21] The compulsive repetition of these traumatic experiences may, to the objective observer, appear as the manifestation of a tendency towards self-destruction. In fact, however, the compulsion to repeat is a desperate attempt to overcome the passivity and helplessness of the original trauma. In this way, the infant acquires an active position, and becomes the subject of its painful experiences instead of their helpless victim.

According to Brunswick, "[T]he child which has just succeeded in the difficult task of reliving actively what it has until now passively experienced—and here the repetition compulsion acquires its full significance—is particularly on the defensive in regard to this freshly acquired activity." (Mack-Brunswick 1950, 267) The child defends its active position first of all against the mother. The mother is not able to recognise that she has become superfluous, and remains active in her care and love of the child. But since the child has acquired the active position, it now resents the activity of the mother,[22] which threatens the active position of the child. According to Brunswick, this is the origin of aggression: "The child reacts to her very presence with a kind of primitive, defensive aggression." (1950, 267) The active mother forces the child back into its original passivity. The child's rage, which is directed against the mother, is ultimately a defence against this original passivity.

Brunswick's reconstruction of the pre-Oedipal phase allows us to explain erotogenic masochism and the origin of aggression. According to Freud, the clearest and most extreme manifestation of erotogenic masochism is the fact that even self-destruction "cannot take place without libidinal satisfaction." (Freud 1924, 170) Freud's reference to a libidinal sympathetic excitation that would accompany everything that occurs in the organism is not very illuminating, however.[23] It begs the question of *how* pleasure can be derived from pain. Brunswick's analysis of the infant's passivity and of its acquisition of an

---

[21] "It can easily be observed that in every field of mental experience, not merely that of sexuality, when a child receives a passive impression it has a tendency to produce an active reaction. It tries to do itself what has just been done to it. This is part of the work imposed on it of mastering the external world and can even lead to its endeavouring to repeat an impression which it would have reason to avoid on account of its distressing content. Children's play, too, is made to serve this purpose of supplementing a passive experience with an active piece of behaviour and of thus, as it were, annulling it." (Freud 1931, 236)

[22] "Any activity on the part of the mother is likely to be resented." (Mack-Brunswick 1950, 267)

[23] "The occurrence of such a libidinal sympathetic excitation when there is tension due to pain and unpleasure would be an infantile physiological mechanism which ceases to operate later on." (Freud 1924, 163)

active position, on the other hand, can help us to explain what Freud calls erotogenic masochism in a different way.

Freud is on the wrong track if he considers masochism as pleasure in pain (*Schmerzlust*);[24] pain itself cannot be a source of pleasure. The "pleasure" of erotogenic masochism is rather in the acquisition of the active position and, therefore, in the triumph over trauma. Given this interpretation of erotogenic masochism, we can understand how there can be a kind of pleasure in self-destruction. The infant actively repeats painful impressions it experienced passively, and though this compulsive repetition of painful experiences gives the impression of being masochistic, it is not, in fact, a search for pleasure in pain. Actively repeating a painful experience is at least an *activity* of the subject and, as such, it is a defence against the original passivity at the time of the trauma. This might explain why self-destruction is preferred over passivity; suicide is, at least, an *act*.

According to Freud, aggression towards external objects must be understood as a deflection of the instinct for self-destruction. In our interpretation of erotogenic masochism, the most primitive source of aggression would be the impotent rage of the infant forced back into its original passivity by the mother, who is unable to abandon the activity the infant needed when it was still passive and helpless. (Mack-Brunswick 1950, 268) After the invention of the *Fort-Da* game, therefore, the constant presence of the mother becomes threatening to the child.

This interpretation of the origin of aggression perfectly matches a phenomenon that puzzled Freud: the negative therapeutic reaction. (Freud 1937, 239) Freud wondered why patients ultimately do not want to be cured, and instead cling to their illness. The patients react in a hostile way to the activity and the correct—all *too* correct—interpretations of the analyst, who forces them into a passive position. The analyst's *furor sanandi* only provokes hostility in his patients, who prefer their own misery to the happiness offered by another. In this connection, it is useful to recall that the negative therapeutic reaction, together with the compulsion to repeat, was one of the phenomena that led Freud to the introduction of the death instinct: "What we are left with is the fact that the organism wishes to die only in its own fashion." (Freud 1920, 39)

The Phallic Mother

Our interpretation of erotogenic masochism as the infant's acquisition of an active position towards painful experiences must also account for another aspect of Freud's theory. According to Freud, the death instinct is at work in *every* organism. Our reference to infantile traumas, on the other hand, seems to introduce an orthopedagogical dimension. At least, it seems to give support to

---

[24] Freud 1924, 163.

the phantasy of a good enough mother who could prevent these traumas, and therefore to the phantasy of the good enough analyst who could cure them.

However, the deficiency of the mother is not accidental. First of all, the helplessness of the infant is also an incapacity to communicate its needs. Therefore, the infant will necessarily experience pain it cannot get rid of immediately. Secondly, the mother should be "bad enough" to allow the child to identify with her and to care for itself. The primitive identification with the mother presupposes an experience of loss of the mother. Freud leaves no doubt that *every* mother is such a "bad enough mother": "The general dissatisfaction of children" shows that the deficiency of the mother is not an accidental, but a *general* one. (Freud 1931, 234) It is merely a function of the infant's radical helplessness.

However, the deficiency of the mother is not just a general one; it is also a *structural* one. In the phallic phase, the child is confronted with the enigma of sexual difference. The genitals of the mother are interpreted as "being castrated". The girl acknowledges this "fact", and will suffer a fatal disappointment that will result in penis envy and a feeling of injustice. The boy, on the other hand, has a double reaction towards the castration of the mother. On the one hand, he will acknowledge the castration of the mother and he will despise her for it. This depreciation of the mother, however, is only the reverse of the boy's own castration anxiety. On the other hand, the boy *disavows* the mother's castration.

In his paper on *Fetishism* (1927), Freud theorises this disavowal as the origin of fetishism. The boy invents a fetish as a substitute for the mother's phallus, and he thus neutralises the possibility of castration.[25] This disavowal of castration is the origin of the phallic mother as a phantasy,[26] and the pre-Oedipal mother is thus not phallic. For the pre-Oedipal infant, sexual difference is not an issue; the phallic mother, on the other hand, is a defence against the possibility of castration. According to Brunswick, "[T]he phallic mother is pure phantasy, a childish hypothesis elaborated after the discovery of the penis and the possibility of its loss or absence in the female. It is a hypothesis made to insure the mother's possession of the penis, and as such probably arises at the moment when the child becomes uncertain that the mother does indeed possess it." (Mack-Brunswick 1950, 270) The phantasy of the phallic mother

---

[25] "The fetish is a substitute for the woman's (the mother's) penis that the little boy once believed in and—for reasons familiar to us—does not want to give up." (Freud 1927, 152)

[26] "In his mind the woman has got a penis, in spite of everything; but this penis is no longer the same as it was before. Something else has taken its place, has been appointed its substitute, as it were, and now inherits the interest which was formerly directed to its predecessor. But this interest suffers an extraordinary increase as well, because the horror of castration has set up a memorial to itself in the creation of this substitute." (Freud 1927, 154)

is a triumph over the threat of castration (Freud 1927, 154), and given that castration, too, is a phantasy, the phallic mother is therefore a phantasy that defends the subject against another phantasy (Rosolato 1967, 9).

In *Fetishism* (1927) and *Splitting of the Ego in the Process of Defence* (1938), Freud describes the dramatic effects on the child's mind of the confrontation with sexual difference (i.e. with the genitals of the mother). According to Freud, this is the most violent trauma of childhood. However, it is difficult to understand why the confrontation with sexual difference would be so disastrous, and Freud's analysis of disavowal in *Splitting of the Ego* enables another interpretation of why the confrontation with the mother's genitals is so important.

In the case of a conflict between an instinctual demand and its prohibition by reality, the child can, according to Freud, react in two ways: it can give in to reality by giving up the demands of the instincts, or it can disavow reality (*die Realität verleugnen*). (Freud 1940, 277) But this alternative only presents itself when the instinct that demands satisfaction is a *sexual* instinct. In the case of hunger, for instance, the infant can hallucinate the image of the mother's breast for a while but, rather quickly, it will have to acknowledge that hunger cannot be satisfied by an image. The instincts of self-preservation cannot be repressed;[27] pain and hunger are imperative. In the absence of the mother, the hungry infant can only panic, and to disavow the danger is therefore only an option in the case of a sexual instinct.

When the boy is confronted with the sight of the female genitals and the threat of castration, he interprets sexual difference as a difference between phallic and castrated. From now on, his own infantile masturbation stands under the threat of castration. In this case, Freud's idea of alternative options holds fast. The boy can acknowledge the danger and give up masturbation, or he can disavow the danger and go on masturbating. The first option will be dominated by the phantasy of castration (neurosis); the second by the phantasy of the phallic mother (homosexuality and fetishism). Of course, we all produce both these phantasies, but it is only the dominance of the one or of the other that will determine if we become neurotics, homosexuals, or fetishists. In homosexuals, the confrontation with sexual difference leads to an *identification* with the phallic mother; in fetishism, the penis of the mother is *substituted* by another part of her body (heterosexuality) or by an inanimate object (perverse fetishism). This substitution "saves the fetishist

---

[27] "Pain is imperative; the only things to which it can yield are removal by some toxic agent or the influence of mental distraction. The case of pain is too obscure to give us any help in our purpose. Let us take the case in which an instinctual stimulus such as hunger remains unsatisfied. It then becomes imperative and can be allayed by nothing but the action that satisfies it. It keeps up a constant tension of need. Nothing in the nature of a repression seems in this case to come remotely into question." (Freud 1915, 146)

from becoming a homosexual, by endowing women with the characteristic which makes them tolerable as sexual objects." (Freud 1927, 154)

Because of the fact that, especially for the child, the sexual instinct does not have the urgency of a vital need, sexuality can become the domain of phantasies and defence-mechanisms. In the domain of self-preservation, they would be vain. This peculiarity of the sexual instinct produces the primacy of sexuality *in phantasy*. Sexuality was the first domain in which our phantasies were of any help to us. The castration of the mother is not a fact, but an interpretation. Therefore, it can become the *pure signal* of danger and the *pure symbol* of the infant's archaic traumas. The relative lack of urgency of the sexual instinct creates the possibility of substitution, identification, and repression[28].

Conclusion

The analysis of female sexuality revealed to Freud that castration is the modification of a more primordial disappointment. Beyond the castration complex are the silent catastrophes of love and need. Our interpretation of Freud's "death-instinct" led us to the discovery of a radical dependence at the heart of the subject. Only from this perspective of radical dependence can we understand the emphasis on primary masochism and fetishism in Freud's later works. Primary masochism and fetishism point to the attempt of the subject to triumph over trauma.

In *Life and Death in Psychoanalysis*, Jean Laplanche writes: "There is a remarkable boldness and a remarkable weakness in the idea that sexuality can *in fact* threaten the life of the child and his self-preservation. What it threatens is indeed a certain integrity, but an integrity which is not *directly* the integrity of life. We should think here of the central role in Freud's theory not of death-anxiety but precisely of castration anxiety as a threat to bodily unity: which is to say that what is threatened, much more than life, is *a certain representation of life*, a certain ideational representative of the vital order." (Laplanche 1985, 49) Our interpretation of castration as a symbolisation of the infant's vital traumas gives a dramatic twist to Laplanche's argument. Indeed, castration is the *representation* of mortal danger; it threatens a certain *representation* of life. But Laplanche does not take into account that this shift to the level of representation is already a modification of a more primordial trauma. Castration anxiety is already an attempt to recover from those mortifications that did not allow for anticipation and anxiety.

---

[28] Pain and hunger cannot be repressed. (Freud 1915, 146)

9. Freud beyond psychoanalysis? (1937)

Analysis terminable and interminable marks a radically new turning point in Freud's thinking, but because it was one of Freud's last works it is never considered as such, except by the Hungarian psychoanalyst, Leopold Szondi. According to Szondi, psychoanalysis (before and after 1937!) neglected the distinction between pathogenesis and aetiology. The reconstruction of the *development* of a psychic illness must be distinguished from its *cause*.[1] This Szondian remark dramatically diminishes the anthropological claims of psychoanalytic interpretation, but Szondi emphasises that he only elaborates Freud's new ideas in *Analysis terminable and interminable*.

1937: Sexualizing psychic conflict?

In "Analysis terminable and interminable" Freud argues that something about the drives themselves resists the permanent and prophylactic cure of neurotic and psychotic suffering. Psychoanalytic technique is unable to alter the constitutional strength of the drives. It remains on the level of psychic representations and their repressions and displacements, and therefore it cannot influence the quantitative aspect of the drives. The pure *intensity* of certain drives is the crucial factor that decides about the form and the degree of psychopathology, and since psychoanalysis only works on the level of psychic representation and only influences the distribution of libido over the representations, it cannot modify the intensity of the drives as such. (1937, 226) This is the reason why Freud hoped that one day psychopharmacology would be able to modify the quantitative aspect, i.e. the intensity, of the drives. (1940, 182) Today we know his hope has not been entirely in vain.

Freud's emphasis on the quantitative aspect of the drives is complemented by a qualitative aspect. Because the drives have different intensities, there will inevitably be a conflict between them. The stronger drives will smother the weaker ones. But, this conflict between the drives with their different intensities is not just a quantitative power play. A qualitative aspect enters into this game: a peculiar *propensity for conflict* ["Konfliktneigung"] between the drives. Different instinctual aims *tend to* conflict with each other. For instance, heterosexual and homosexual impulses fight one another in such a way that the strongest impulse will inhibit and repress the other *completely*. According to

---

[1] Die Psychoanalyse hat die Grenzen zwischen Krankheitsentwicklung und Krankheitsursache zu wenig beachtet. Eine Entwicklungsgeschichte mit den einleuchtendsten Konstruktionen der Pathogenese darf niemals mit der urtümlichen Ursache einer Krankheit verwechselt werden. (Szondi 1963, 58)

Freud, this is not just the result of the quantitative differences in strength between the drives:

> "We might attempt to explain this by saying that each individual only has a certain quota of libido at his disposal, for which the two rival trends have to struggle. But it is not clear why the rivals do not always divide up the available quota of libido between them according to their *relative* strength, since they are able to do so in a number of cases. We are forced to the conclusion that the tendency to a conflict is something special, something which is newly added to the situation, irrespective of the quantity of libido." (1937, 244, my italics)

Although we all have a bisexual constitution, few of us will succeed in becoming hetero- *and* homosexual. Because of the propensity for conflict between the drives, the stronger heterosexuality will repress the weaker homosexuality *completely* and we will become *exclusive* heterosexuals, or vice versa. Apparently, it is very hard to experience the diversity of drives as anything else than as an opposition between the drives.

This is a remarkable turn in Freud's thinking because he always maintained that not the conflict between the drives, but the ego's defence against the drives causes repression. In the analysis of the Wolfman, Freud says that psychic conflict should not be understood as a conflict between two sexual drives, but as a conflict between the ego and the sexual drive:

> "Conflicts between sexuality and the moral ego trends are far more common than such as take place within the sphere of sexuality. To insist that bisexuality is the motive force leading to repression is to take too narrow a view; whereas if we assert the same of the conflict between the ego and the sexual tendencies (that is, the libido) we shall have covered all possible cases." (1918, 110)

In the same passage, he even claims that "the ego has no sexual currents, but only an interest in its own self-protection and in the preservation of its narcissism." (1918, 112) So, when Freud introduces the idea of a fundamental conflict between different sexual drives in "Analysis terminable and interminable", he thereby proposes a radical revision of the psychoanalytic theory of psychic conflict. According to Freud, "the question at once arises whether all that we know about psychical conflict should not be revised from this new angle." (1937, 244) Maybe the fundamental and original psychic conflict is *not between a non-sexual ego and the libido, but between different sexual drives*. To understand Freud's question whether "all that we know about psychical conflict should not be revised from this new angle," we will first take a closer look at his own earlier refutation of this sexualization of psychic conflict.

1919: A critique of Freud's critique of Fliess

In "A child is being beaten" Freud criticizes the theory of repression proposed by Wilhelm Fliess. This theory takes as its starting point the constitutional bisexuality of all human beings. This bisexual disposition will lead in most people (those who do not become manifest bisexuals) to a conflict between their heterosexual and their homosexual impulses. The stronger impulse will then repress the other. Clearly, this is the same conception of psychic conflict as the one Freud presents in "Analysis terminable and interminable." But in 1919, Freud still maintained that such a conflict between two sexual drives cannot explain repression and the pathologies that result from it. To understand his argument, we will briefly summarize his analysis of masochism in "A child is being beaten" and then we will return to his critique of Fliess.

In "A child is being beaten" Freud discusses a few of his patients whose sexual lives were more or less absorbed by the sexual phantasy that a child is being beaten. This phantasy was cathected with a high degree of pleasure. Furthermore, these patients were all rather hesitant to confess this phantasy to their analyst. But, what surprises Freud most is the fact that this sexual phantasy is very vague and anonymous. None of these patients could identify the people in the phantasy and they could not say which position they themselves took in the phantasy: "Only the hesitant reply: '*a* child is being beaten... It doesn't matter which'." (1919, 181, my italics) Freud considers this vagueness and anonymity of the phantasy as a symptom, or more correctly, as a sign that something is repressed, and this allows him to propose a construction about the psychogenesis of this phantasy.

According to Freud, the sexual phantasy that a child is being beaten originates from a libidinal attachment to the father. The child wants to be loved by the father and preferred by him over its siblings. This results in the wishful phantasy: "My father loves only me, not the other child." In the oedipal phase, this wish becomes invested with genital libido and becomes an incestuous genital phantasy. Because of the incest taboo and the castration complex, this phantasy is repressed. But, the child now finds a regressive substitute: "I want to be loved by my father" is transformed into the masochistic phantasy "I want to be *beaten* by my father". This masochistic phantasy is the regressive substitute for the incestuous genital phantasy as well as the expression of the punishment for engaging in it. According to Freud, this masochistic phantasy "I am being beaten by my father" is the repressed kernel behind the vague and anonymous phantasy that *a* child is being beaten.

What is important for understanding Freud's critique of Fliess is that this psychogenesis of masochism applies to both men and women: "In both cases the beating-phantasy has its origin in an incestuous attachment to the father." (1919, 198) According to Freud, this is a fundamental argument against Fliess's theory. At first sight, Fliess's bisexual theory of repression seems to hold in the case of men. Indeed, in Freud's analysis, the masochistic phantasy originates from the repression of the feminine position towards the father. But, in the case of women, it is the same feminine position that is repressed. In their case, too, the sexual attachment to the father is repressed although this sexual attachment to the father is in accordance with their anatomical sex:

> "There can be no doubt that the original phantasy in the case of the girl, 'I am being beaten (i.e. I am loved) by my father', represents a feminine attitude, and corresponds to her dominant and manifest sex; according to the [Fliess's] theory, therefore, it ought to escape repression, and there would be no need for its becoming unconscious. But as a matter of fact it does become unconscious." (1919, 202)

For Freud, this is a decisive argument against Fliess's theory of repression, and against any theory that considers the fundamental psychic conflict as a conflict between different sexual trends, and not as a conflict between sexuality, on the one hand, and the ego, on the other: "The theory of psychoanalysis (a theory based on observation) holds firmly to the view that the motive forces of repression must not be sexualized." (1919, 203)

However, Freud's appeal to observation is not as convincing as that. In Freud's own text, we find some elements to problematize his critique of Fliess. We will first point out four problems which threaten to undermine Freud's analysis of masochism and his critique of Fliess, and then we will discuss Freud's surprising answer to these problems.

First problem: To be able to criticize Fliess's bisexual theory of repression, Freud has to appeal to the un-psychoanalytic, popular opinion that the dominant sexual drive corresponds to the manifest, anatomical sex. Freud says about Fliess's theory that "such a theory as this can only have an intelligible meaning if we assume that a person's sex is to be determined by the formation of his genitals; for otherwise it would not be certain which is a person's stronger sex." (1919, 201) Like Fliess's theory, Freud's argument against it suffers from a confusion between sexual identity and sexual orientation, or between homosexuality and transsexualism. Therefore, it is not clear whether it is about a conflict between homosexual and heterosexual trends or a conflict between maleness and femaleness. In both cases, however, Freud's argument does not hold. With regard to sexual object choice, it is obvious that this does not depend on the person's manifest, anatomical sex, quite simply because homosexuality exists, and when we take into consideration what we now know about transsexualism, Freud's argument makes no sense either. A person's sex cannot be determined solely by the formation of his genitals, and it is therefore not certain which a person's stronger sex is. (Stoller 1984, 39) But this does not imply that there cannot be a fundamental conflict between male and female impulses, a conflict which would lead to the repression of one of these impulses, even regardless of the anatomical sex. On the contrary, the more we know about homosexuality and about transsexualism, the more likely it becomes that there are such fundamental conflicts between hetero- and homosexual impulses and, more fundamentally, between the sense of maleness and the sense of femaleness. (See: Stoller 1984)

Second problem: Freud says in "A child is being beaten" that the phantasy "I am being beaten (i.e. I am loved) by my father" is repressed and becomes unconscious. (1919, 203) But, in this, Freud takes his wishes for reality. In fact, this "unconscious phantasy" is Freud's own construction, and he is very explicit about this: "It has never had a real existence. It is never remembered, it has never succeeded in becoming conscious. It is a construction of analysis." (1919, 185) Freud's patients only express the phantasy that "*a* child is being beaten". But, why would this be the result of repression? This anonymous and vague phantasy is "cathected with a high degree of pleasure" (1919, 180) which would be quite remarkable if it were a symptom and a defence against the return of the repressed. A symptom is by definition an equivalent of anxiety and inhibition, which seem absent in the masochistic pleasures of Freud's patients.

Third problem: In "A child is being beaten" Freud says that his patients' masochism cannot be understood as an element of their neurosis: "The analytic physician is obliged to admit to himself that to a great extent these phantasies subsist apart from the rest of the content of a neurosis, and find no proper place in its structure. But impressions of this kind, as I know from my own experience, are only too willingly put on one side." (1919, 183) Apparently, Freud immediately forgot his own warning, because he never addresses this problem in his analysis of masochism.

Fourth problem: The most abstract but maybe the most important problem with Freud's analysis of masochism is, as he admits himself, that it is too general. Freud's analysis of masochism does not explain why *only* masochism could be the outcome of the factors that are supposed to determine it. The same factors (Oedipus complex, repression, regression, etc.) could have produced homosexuality, perversion or any kind of psychoneurosis. (Dayan 1985, 318-325) In "A child is being beaten" Freud minimizes this problem by saying that "we ought to be content to explain the facts before us, and ought as a rule to avoid the additional task of making it clear why something has *not* taken place." (1919, 183) However, this epistemological modesty falls short of Freud's own scientific ideals and especially of his adherence to determinism. To explain why something did *not* take place is not an *additional* task; it is a necessary element of every deterministic explanation of "the facts before us". This is a serious problem for the scientific status of psychoanalytic psychopathology because Freud's theory is unable to determine *specific aetiologies* and therefore remains on the level of occasional causes. (Szondi 1963, 87) Still today, this problem provokes confusion in the quarrels between psychoanalysis and biological and evolutionary psychiatry. Biological psychiatry does not (in principle) deny the influence of the environment and early life-history, but it maintains—correctly—that these factors never reveal *specific* aetiologies.

These four problems are not just external objections to psychoanalytic theory. In "Analysis terminable and interminable" Freud himself is still preoccupied with them. But before we return to 1937, we will first discuss a text which anticipates the concerns expressed in "Analysis terminable and interminable" and which deals extensively with the four problems we have mentioned above: "The psychogenesis of a case of homosexuality in a woman" (1920).

1920: The "analysis" of a healthy girl

"The psychogenesis of a case of homosexuality in a woman" is a peculiar work. At first sight it appears as a typical oedipal interpretation of homosexuality, exactly like Freud's psychogenesis of masochism in "A child is being beaten". But, at the same time, it is the text in which Freud most radically problematizes the basic assumptions of psychoanalysis and in which he seems to anticipate his proposal of 1937 to sexualize psychic conflict and to emphasize the importance of constitution as the dominant aetiological factor.

A beautiful and clever girl of eighteen is sent to Freud by her parents because she has fallen in love with an older woman who, "in spite of her distinguished name, is nothing but a *cocotte*." (1920, 147) The girl is so madly in love with her lady that she is willing to lie and cheat to be able to meet her and that she loses all interest in her schoolwork and her friends. At a certain moment, while she is walking through town with her lady, they bump into her father who passes them by with an angry glance. When the lady hears that this man is the girl's father, she tells the girl that the affair must come to an end. Afraid that she will never see her loved one again, the girl jumps over a wall down the side of a cutting on to the suburban railway line which ran close by. Freud repeatedly emphasizes the seriousness of this suicide attempt. (1920, 147-148 and 161) After this attempt at suicide, her parents send her to Freud to be "cured".

On the basis of the girl's story, Freud proposes a construction about the psychogenesis of her homosexuality. He builds his construction on the fact that the girl became an overt homosexual at sixteen, at the time her mother gave birth to a little boy. From this, Freud concludes:

> "It was just when the girl was experiencing the revival of her infantile Oedipus complex at puberty that she suffered her great disappointment. She became keenly conscious of the wish to have a child, and a male one; that what she desired was her *father's* child and an image of *him*, her consciousness was not allowed to know. And what happened next? It was not *she* who bore the child, but her unconsciously hated rival, her mother. Furiously resentful and embittered, she turned away from her father and from men altogether. After this first great reverse she forswore her womanhood and sought another goal for her libido." (1920, 157)

As with the masochistic phantasy we discussed above, Freud analyzes the girl's homosexuality as a defence against and a substitute for the impossible oedipal attachment to the father. Freud highlights that this construction is not just "a product of my inventive powers; it is based on such trustworthy analytic evidence that I can claim objective validity for it." (1920, 156) We have no reason to doubt it, but then the same problems that we already discussed in the case of his construction about the psychogenesis of masochism return again in this case. This time, however, Freud deals with these problems explicitly. At first, Freud starts to wonder about the validity of his construction because, when he tells it to the girl, it does not impress her at all: "She replied in an inimitable tone, 'How very interesting', as though she were a *grande dame* being taken over a museum and glancing through her *lorgnon* at objects to which she was completely indifferent." (1920, 163) Such an indifference towards an oedipal interpretation of one's symptoms might be common today, now that people come into analysis with the *expectation* to get such an interpretation from the analyst, but it is rather surprising in the case of a young girl in the 1910s, who "was by no means lacking in a sense of decency and propriety." (1920, 147) In any case, the girl's natural indifference to Freud's construction makes him wonder.

In response to the girl's indifference, Freud starts to question the most basic assumptions of his theory. First of all, he comes back to the problem of specific aetiologies (see above: fourth problem). The construction about the genesis of homosexuality appears to give a causal explanation of how the girl's heterosexual attachment to her father is transformed into her manifest homosexuality. But, Freud now admits that other things could have happened as a response to the disappointment by the father. Why did the girl "choose" homosexuality, and not masochism or neurosis as an answer to this oedipal trauma? Although only a year before, in "A child is being beaten", Freud was still convinced that we better neglect this problem, now he admits that there is indeed a weak point in his causal explanations:

> "So long as we trace the development from its final outcome backwards, the chain of events appears continuous, and we feel we have gained an insight which is completely satisfactory or even exhaustive. But if we proceed the reverse way, if we start from the premises inferred from the analysis and try to follow these up to the final result, then we no longer get the impression of an inevitable sequence of events which could not have been otherwise determined. We notice at once that there might have been another result, and that we might have been just as well able to understand and explain the latter. The synthesis is thus not so satisfactory as the analysis." (1920, 167)

In other words, psychoanalysis cannot explain why in this case *only* homosexuality could have been the outcome. The reconstruction of the psychogenesis does not provide a specific aetiology. To understand why the girl responded to the oedipal trauma with becoming homosexual, Freud has to appeal to internal, constitutional factors.[2] The girl became homosexual in response to the oedipal trauma *because she was always already homosexual*.

---

[2] "There must have been present in this girl special factors that turned the scale, factors outside the trauma, probably of an internal nature." (1920, 168)

According to Freud, all human beings are constitutionally bisexual. (1920, 157) The girl became a manifest homosexual because her homosexual drive has always been much stronger than the heterosexual impulse:

> "From very early years, her libido had flowed in two currents, the one on the surface being one that we may unhesitatingly designate as homosexual. This latter was probably a *direct* and *unchanged* continuation of an infantile fixation on her mother." (1920, 168)

In this passage, Freud anticipates his remark in "Analysis terminable and interminable" that there is a fundamental conflict between the heterosexual and the homosexual impulse and that — because of the propensity for conflict — the stronger drive will repress the other completely.[3] This implies, first of all, that the girl's homosexuality is not the outcome of the oedipal crisis and that it is thus not a defensive reaction against a traumatic experience. On the contrary, the girl's homosexuality is a spontaneous, non-reactive expression of her sexual drive. This is the reason why her homosexuality cannot be analyzed and why she reacts so indifferently to Freud's interpretation: there is simply nothing to be analyzed because her homosexuality is an unchanged and direct expression of the homosexual drive which always already dominated her conscious life. But then what is the status of Freud's oedipal construction about the psychogenesis of homosexuality? Did Freud not say that this interpretation "is based on such trustworthy analytic evidence that I can claim objective validity for it"? (1920, 156) To solve this problem, Freud makes a remarkable claim which radically changes the position of the unconscious for the understanding of human nature. Freud writes:

> "Possibly the analysis described here actually revealed nothing more than the process by which, on an appropriate occasion, the deeper heterosexual current of libido, too, was deflected into the manifest homosexual one." (1920, 169)

Freud suggests here that his "psychogenesis of homosexuality" does not explain how this girl became homosexual, but only how her unconscious heterosexuality was transformed into homosexuality in such a way that it was able to re-enforce her already manifest homosexuality. Thanks to this unconscious process, she overcame the conflict between her dominant homosexuality and her unconscious heterosexuality. This is the reason why, as Freud repeatedly stresses, "the girl was not in any way ill (she did not suffer from anything in herself, nor did she complain of her condition)." (1920, 150)

In 1920, Freud already anticipated his suggestion in "Analysis terminable and interminable" to revise the theory of psychic conflict. The only way to understand the "analysis" of this healthy homosexual girl, is to think about

---

[3] "Presages of later homosexuality had always occupied her *conscious* life, while the attitude arising from the Oedipus complex had remained *unconscious* and had appeared only in such signs as her tender behaviour to the little boy." (1920, 168, italics in the original)

psychic conflict, not as a conflict between the ego and the libido, but as a conflict between two sexual currents. In all human beings, there is a conflict between heterosexual and homosexual impulses. The stronger impulse will inhibit and repress the other completely. The repressed impulse will then return from the unconscious as a neurotic symptom or it will be transformed in such a way that it becomes a re-enforcement of the dominant impulse, as in the fortunate case of the homosexual girl.

In 1920, Freud already suggests that it might be necessary to sexualize the theory of psychic conflict, something he still resisted vehemently in 1919. This sexualization of psychic conflict can also solve the problems we detected in "A child is being beaten".

"A child is being beaten" revisited

We argued above that Freud's psychogenesis of masochism in "A child is being beaten" was too general. Freud seems to give a deterministic causal explanation, but he admits immediately that other things might have happened and that he would have been able to explain these other things just as well (*fourth problem*). To explain that *only* masochism could be the outcome, he has to turn to constitutional factors. As in the case of homosexuality, Freud would have to postulate a "direct and unchanged" masochism, which originates independent of the oedipal problematic. This reference to a spontaneous, constitutional masochism as the determining aetiological factor also solves the other problems we mentioned above.

In 1919, Freud considers the phantasy that 'a child is being beaten' as a symptom or as the result of the repression of the phantasy that 'I am being beaten (I am loved) by my father.' We already pointed to the problem that a symptom which is not accompanied by inhibitions and anxiety and which is cathected with a high degree of pleasure is not really a symptom (*second problem*). And indeed, why should the impersonal and anonymous character of the phantasy ('*a* child is being beaten') be a signal of repression? Are impersonality and anonymity not rather the qualities of the sexual drive as such? (Deleuze 1993, 13) The dominant drives dominate the ego, but this does not imply that they become 'personal'. For instance, one does not become a manifest homosexual because one's ego identifies with the homosexual drive. On the contrary, the dominant homosexual drive identifies the ego as homosexual. Or, as Freud says about the homosexual girl: "She said she could not conceive of any other way of being in love." (1920, 153) The (dominant) drives are about destiny, not about psychology.

This emphasis on the spontaneous and impersonal character of the dominant drives also explains why the masochism of Freud's patients "subsists apart from the rest of the content of a neurosis, and finds no proper place in its structure" (*third problem*). Their masochism is not the result of an oedipal trauma; it is a spontaneous and unchanged force.[4] Their neuroses on the other hand result from the return of other, unconscious drives.

Four kinds of psychic conflict

The case of the homosexual girl shows that to think psychic conflict as a conflict between the ego and the libido is inadequate. Such conflicts must further be analyzed in terms of a more fundamental conflict between two sexual tendencies. But, then a new question arises. How many of such conflicts and how many tendencies must we distinguish? Of course, this is a very fundamental and general question that cannot be decided here, but the texts we have discussed can help us to distinguish different levels of psychic conflict.

First of all, there is the conflict between heterosexual and homosexual impulses. In 1937 and in the case study of the homosexual girl in 1920, Freud acknowledges that this seems to be an original conflict *within* the sphere of sexuality. The case of the homosexual girl shows that, if one can solve this conflict, one does not suffer from anything in one self. (1920, 150) Therefore, this case indicates that the conflict between hetero- and homosexuality is a fundamental conflict in neurosis.

This conflict on the level of sexual object choice must be distinguished from another and more fundamental conflict on the level of sexual identity: the conflict between the sense of maleness and the sense of femaleness. In 1920, Freud emphasizes this distinction and he points to the confusion between homosexuality and transsexualism in the works of his contemporaries and in his own earlier works:

> "The literature of homosexuality usually fails to distinguish clearly enough between questions of the choice of an object on the one hand, and of the sexual characteristics and the sexual attitude of the subject on the other, as though the answer to the former necessarily involved the answers to the latter." (1920, 170)

Freud himself failed to distinguish homosexuality and transsexualism in the analysis of Schreber. Freud speaks about Schreber's "homosexuality" that is repressed and transformed into delusions of persecution. But Freud's conclusion that Schreber suffers from repressed homosexuality is based on Schreber's

---

[4] Krafft-Ebing, too, already emphasized that masochism is not motivated by a reaction or a defence against the genital drive. About the "psychic impotence" of masochists he writes in his *Psychopathia sexualis*: "*Diese psychische Impotenz beruht dann aber durchaus nicht etwa auf einem horror sexus alterius, sondern nur darauf, dass dem perversen Triebe eine andere Befriedigung als die normale, zwar auch durch das Weib, aber nicht durch Koitus,* adäquat *ist.*" (1997, 105, my italics) Masochists are not interested in genital satisfaction, not because they are afraid of it, but because their sexuality is expressed *adequately* in their masochistic activities.

account of a transsexual dream in which he desired 'to be a woman'. (1911, 13) Because of this confusion in Freud's analysis, he is not able to explain the specific aetiology of Schreber's psychosis. Why would repressed homosexuality result in paranoia and not in neurosis, masochism, or another pathology? Freud does not understand Schreber's paranoia as the result of a conflict between his manifest sense of maleness and the repressed femaleness that is expressed in his delusions. (Stoller 1984, 153-154) Freud confuses homosexuality and transsexualism and therefore he cannot explain why a problem on the level of sexual object choice would lead to a disorder of (sexual) *identity*.

How does masochism fit into this sexual model of psychic conflict? Can we describe sadism and masochism as expressions of bisexuality on the level of the sexual *aim*? Freud and Krafft-Ebing sometimes think sadism as an exaggeration of male sexuality and masochism as an exaggeration of female sexuality (Krafft-Ebing 1997, 151 and Freud 1905, 160), but this seems not much more that an ideological construction. It also contradicts Freud's later idea that men love according to the anaclitic type, which implies idealisation of and submission to the loved one. (1914, 88) The conflict between sadism and masochism can, in our opinion, only be considered as an original conflict, which cannot be derived from the bisexual constitution of human beings as such. Another advantage of thinking the conflict between sadism and masochism as an *original* conflict is that it can integrate Deleuze's discovery that masochism is an original and independent instinctual tendency, and that it is thus not a sadism turned round upon oneself. (Deleuze 1991, 43-45) Maybe there exists a masochism that is a transformed sadism, but then this is only the result of the unconscious process to bring the repressed sadism in accordance with the manifest and unchanged masochism. This conflict between sadism and masochism can also explain why three of the six masochists in "A child is being beaten" were obsessional neurotics. (1919, 182) Obsessional symptoms are the return of repressed sadism.

The case of the homosexual girl allows us to distinguish a fourth level of psychic conflict, i.e. a conflict on the level of the *affects*. In his account of this case, Freud stresses the seriousness of her attempt at suicide (1920, 161), her suppressed rage against her father (1920, 163), and the lack of any sign of hysteria (1920, 155). But, what is the connection between the seriousness of her *passage à l'acte*, the suppressed rage and the absence of hysteria? Freud does not make this connection but the theory of the Hungarian psychopathologist Leopold Szondi allows us to make sense of it. Szondi has modernized the ancient Greek idea that epilepsy is the male counterpart of hysteria. According to Szondi, the epileptic seizure has to do with the suppression of male affects such as rage, while the hysterical fit is the discharge of suppressed female affects. (Szondi 1952, 90) The normal equivalents of epilepsy are revolt and rage; the normal equivalent of hysteria is persuasion by tears. This conflict between 'epilepsy' and 'hysteria' can elucidate the homosexual girl's affective attitude. The "seriousness" of her suicide attempt indicates that it is closer to an epileptic than to a hysterical attack: It is clearly a displaced discharge of the suppressed *rage* against her father. This 'propensity for the epileptic' could also account for the absence of hysteria in her case. She reacts to her father's orders with sound and fury, not with tears and complaints. According to Szondi, this conflict between epilepsy and hysteria, or between "too much anger and too many tears" (Scott Fitzgerald), is an original conflict innate in all of us.

Conclusion

These four levels of conflict between different sexual drives present a complicated version of Fliess's bisexual theory of psychic conflict and repression, and as such this model develops Freud's suggestion in 1937 to 'sexualize' psychic conflict and to stress the importance of constitutional factors. Such a sophisticated return to Fliess has some significant advantages over the classical model of psychic conflict as a conflict between an a-sexual ego and the libido. Freud's sustained refusal to sexualize psychic conflict led him into theoretical impasses which made his metapsychology untenable. The most important impasse is the idea of an ego which has no sexual currents (1918, 112) and whose only aim consists in the radical extinction of any instinctual tension (1915, 120). In a sexual model of psychic conflict, on the other hand, the ego is merely the *locus* of the dominant drives. These dominant drives are not directed towards discharge of tension but towards pleasure. Only the repressed impulses behave like Freudian drives: They express themselves in unconscious phantasies, symptoms and anxiety, they are experienced as compulsive and they only search for discharge of tension. The other, dominant drives, on the other hand, seek for application in life; they are pure positivities enjoying their own strength and they are not experienced as compulsive, as is made clear by Freud's homosexual girl.

In *Analysis terminable and interminable*, Freud leaves us with a plea for theoretical and therapeutic modesty: Psychoanalysis deals with the *historical* vicissitudes of the drives, but these vicissitudes are only the historical and personal reflection of an impersonal and anonymous instinctual *destiny* (*Triebschicksal*).

REFERENCES

ABRAHAM, K. (1949). Remarks on the Psycho-Analysis of a Case of Foot and Corset Fetishism. *Selected Papers of Karl Abraham*. London: Hogarth, pp. 125-136.

ABRAHAM, N. (1987). Le symbole ou l'au-delà du phénomène. ABRAHAM, N. & TOROK, M. *L'écorce et le noyau*. Paris: Flammarion, pp. 25-76.

ASSOUN, P.L. (1981). *Introduction à l'épistemologie freudienne*. Paris: Payot.

BADCOCK, Ch. (1991). *Evolution and Individual Behaviour: an introduction to human sociobiology*. Oxford: Blackwell.

BEARD, G.M. (1999). *La neurasthénie sexuelle*. Paris: L'Harmattan.

BERNET, R. (2000). Le sujet traumatisé. *Revue de métaphysique et de morale* 2: 141-161.

BION, W. (1962). *Learning from experience*. London: Karnac.

—. (1967). *Second Thoughts*. London: Karnac.

—. (1970). *Attention and Interpretation*. London: Karnac.

BIRCH, P. (1999). *Bad Penny*. London: Nexus.

BOLLAS, Ch. (2000). *Hysteria*. London: Routledge.

BOWLBY, J. (1969). *Attachment and Loss, vol.1: Attachment*. New York: Basic Books.

—. (1973). *Attachment and Loss, vol.2: Separation, Anxiety and Anger*. New York: Basic Books.

BURKE, E. (1998). *A Philosophical Enquiry into the Sublime and Beautiful*. London: Penguin.

DARWIN, Ch. (1989). *The Descent of Man, and Selection in Relation to Sex*. London: Pickering.

DAYAN, M. (1985). *Inconscient et réalité*. Paris: PUF

DEAN, C. et al. (2001). Growth processes in teeth distinguish modern humans from Homo erectus and earlier hominins. *Nature* 414: 628-631.

DELEUZE, G. (1967). *Présentation de Sacher-Masoch*. Paris: Minuit

—. (1993). *Critique et Clinique*. Paris: Minuit.

DIAMOND, J. (2002). *The Rise and Fall of the Third Chimpanzee*. London: Vintage.

FERENCZI, S. (1999). Two Types of War Neuroses. *Selected Writings*. London: Penguin, pp. 129-144.

—. (1982). Réflexions sur le traumatisme. *Psychanalyse IV. Oeuvres complètes* 1927-1933, pp.139-147.

FLIESS, W. (1977). *Les relations entre le nez et les organes génitaux féminins présentées selon leurs significations biologiques*. Paris: Seuil.

FONAGY, P. (2001). *Attachment Theory and Psychoanalysis*. New York: Other Press

FREUD, S. (1966). *The Standard Edition of the Complete Psychological Works of Sigmund Freud*. 24 vol.(ed. J. Strachey) London: Hogarth.
FREUD, S. & BREUER, J. (1895). *Studies on Hysteria*. S.E.2.
FREUD, S. (1894). The Neuro-Psychoses of Defence. S.E. 3.
—. (1895). On the grounds for detaching a particular syndrome from neurasthenia under the description 'anxiety neurosis'. S.E. 3.
—. (1896). Further Remarks on the Neuro-Psychoses of Defence. S.E. 3.
—. (1896). The Aetiology of Hysteria. S.E. 3.
—. (1898). Sexuality in the Aetiology of the Neuroses. S.E. 3.
—. (1900). *The Interpretation of Dreams*. S.E. 4-5.
—. (1905). *Three Essays on the Theory of Sexuality*. S.E. 7.
—. (1905). Fragment of an Analysis of a Case of Hysteria. S.E.7.
—. (1905). *Jokes and their Relation to the Unconscious*. S.E. 8.
—. (1906). My Views on the Part played by Sexuality in the Aetiology of the Neuroses. S.E. 7.
—. (1908). On the Sexual Theories of Children. S.E. 9.
—. (1908). Creative Writers and Day-Dreaming. S.E. 9.
—. (1909). Analysis of a Phobia in a Five-Year-Old Boy. S.E. 10.
—. (1909). Notes upon a Case of Obsessional Neurosis. S.E. 10.
—. (1910). *Leonardo da Vinci and a Memory of his Childhood*. S.E. 11.
—. (1911). Psycho-Analytic Notes on an Autobiographical Account of a Case of Paranoia (Dementia Paranoides). S.E. 12.
—. (1912). On the Universal Tendency to Debasement in the Sphere of Love. S.E. 11.
—. (1912-13). *Totem and Taboo*. S.E. 13.
—. (1914). On Narcissism: an Introduction. S.E. 14.
—. (1914). Remembering, Repeating and Working-Through (Further Recommendations on the Technique of Psycho-Analysis). S.E. 12.
—. (1915). Instincts and their Vicissitudes. S.E. 14.
—. (1915). Repression. S.E. 14.
—. (1915). The Unconscious. S.E. 14.
—. (1917). A Metapsychological Supplement to the Theory of Dreams. S.E. 14.
—. (1917). On Transformations of Instinct as Exemplified in Anal Erotism. S.E. 17.
—. (1918). From the History of an Infantile Neurosis. S.E. 17.
—. (1919). A Child is Being Beaten. S.E. 17.
—. (1920). *Beyond the Pleasure Principle*. S.E. 18.
—. (1920). The psychogenesis of a case of homosexuality in a woman. S.E. 18
—. (1923). *The Ego and the Id*. S.E. 19.
—. (1923). The Infantile Genital Organization. S.E. 19.
—. (1924). The Economic Problem of Masochism. S.E. 19.
—. (1924). The Dissolution of the Oedipus Complex. S.E. 19.

—. (1925). Some Psychical Consequences of the Anatomical Distinction between the Sexes. *S.E.* 19.
—. (1926). *Inhibitions, Symptoms and Anxiety. S.E.* 20.
—. (1926). *The Question of Lay Analysis. S.E.* 20.
—. (1927). Fetishism. *S.E.* 21.
—. (1930). *Civilization and its Discontents. S.E.* 21.
—. (1931). Female Sexuality. *S.E.* 21.
—. (1933). *New Introductory Lectures on Psycho-Analysis. S.E.* 22.
—. (1937). Analysis Terminable and Interminable. *S.E.* 23.
—. (1939). *Moses and Monotheism. S.E.* 23.
—. (1940). *An Outline of Psycho-Analysis. S.E.* 23.
—. (1940). Splitting of the Ego in the Process of Defence. *S.E.* 23.
—. (1966). Project for a scientific psychology. *S.E.* 1.
—. (1975). *Minutes of the Vienna Psycho-Analytic Society, Vol.IV (1912–1918).* New York: International Universities Press.
—. (1985). *The Complete Letters of Sigmund Freud to Wilhelm Fliess*, Cambridge, MA: Harvard University Press.
—. (1986). *Briefe an Wilhelm Fliess.* Frankfurt am Main: Fischer.
FREUD, S. & ABRAHAM, K. (1965). *A Psycho-Analytic Dialogue: The Letters of Sigmund Freud and Karl Abraham 1907–1926.* London: Hogarth.
GAY, P. (1989). *Freud. A Life for our Time.* New York: Anchor Books.
GEYSKENS, T. (2001). Freud's Letters to Fliess. From Seduction to Sexual Biology, From Psychopathology to a Clinical Anthropology. *International Journal of Psycho-Analysis*, 82: 861–876.
—. (2003). Imre Hermann's Freudian theory of attachment. *International Journal of Psycho-Analysis*, 84: 1517-1529
—. & VAN HAUTE, Ph. (2003). *Van doodsdrift tot hechtingstheorie. Het primaat van het kind bij Freud, Klein en Hermann.* Amsterdam: Boom.
GREEN, A. (1997). *Les chaînes d'Eros. Actualité du sexuel.* Paris: Odile Jacob.
—. (2000). *La diachronie en psychanalyse.* Paris: Minuit.
—. (2000a). *Le temps éclaté.* Paris Minuit.
HAECKEL, E. (1910). *Anthropogenie oder Entwickelungsgeschichte des Menschen.* Leipzig: Engelmann.
ISAACS, S. (1991). The nature and function of phantasy. *The Freud-Klein Controversies 1941-1945.* London: Routledge and Kegan Paul.
JUNG, C.G. (1956). *Symbols of Transformation: an analysis of the prelude to a case of schizophrenia. Collected Works 5.* London: Routledge and Kegan Paul.
JURIST, E. et al. (2002). *Affect Regulation, Mentalization, and the Development of the Self.* New York: Other Press.
KERNBERG, O. (1991). A Contemporary Reading of "On Narcissism". in SANDLER, J. *Freud's "On Narcissism: An Introduction".* New Haven & London: Yale University Press, pp. 131-148.

KLEIN, M. (1997). On mental health. *Envy and Gratitude and other works 1946-1963*. London: Vintage, pp. 268-274.

KRAFFT-EBING, R. von. (1997). *Psychopathia sexualis*. München: Matthes & Seitz Verlag.

LAPLANCHE, J. (1980a). *Problématique 1. L'angoisse*. Paris: PUF.

—. (1980b). *Problématique 2. Castration. Symbolisation*. Paris: PUF.

—. (1985). *Life and Death in Psychoanalysis*. Baltimore: John Hopkins University Press.

—. (1994). *Nouveaux fondements pour la psychanalyse*. Paris: Quadrige/PUF.

—. & PONTALIS, J.B. (1988). *The Language of Psychoanalysis*. London: Karnac.

—. & PONTALIS, J.B. (1985). *Fantasme originaire, fantasmes des origines, origines du fantasme*. Paris: Hachette.

LECLAIRE, S. (1968). *Psychanalyser*. Paris: Seuil.

LURIA, A. (1973). *The Working Brain. An Introduction to Neuropsychology*. London: Penguin.

MACK-BRUNSWICK, R. (1928). Die Analyse eines Eifersuchtswahnes. *Intern. Zeitschr. für Psychoanalyse*, pp. 458-507.

—. (1950). The Pre-Oedipal Phase of Libido Development. *The Psychoanalytic Reader*. London: Hogarth, pp. 231-253.

MASSON, J. (1984). *The Assault on Truth: Freud's Suppression of the Seduction Theory*. New York: Farrar Straus & Giroux.

MAY, U. (1999). Freud's early clinical theory and historiography. *Int. J. Psychoanal.*, 80: 769-81.

McDOUGALL, J.(1980). *Plea for a Measure of Abnormality*. New York: Int. Univ. Press.

—. (1995). *The Many Faces of Eros: A psychoanalytic exploration of human sexuality*. New York: Norton.

MACGUIRE, W. (ed.) (1974). *The Freud/Jung Letters: the correspondence between Sigmund Freud and C.G. Jung*. London: Hogarth.

M'UZAN, M. de. (1977). Un cas de masochisme pervers. Esquisse d'une théorie. *De l'art à la mort*. Paris: Gallimard, pp. 125-150.

NANCY, J-L. (1993). In Statu Nascendi. *The Birth to Presence*. Stanford: Stanford University Press, pp. 211–233.

PINKER, S. (1998). *How the Mind Works*. London: Penguin.

RANK, O. (1924). *Das Trauma der Geburt*. Vienna: Int. Psych.An. Verlag.

RICHARDS, A. (1996). Ladies of Fashion: Pleasure, Perversion or Paraphilia. *Int. Journ. of Psycho-Analysis* 77: 337-351.

RIDLEY, M. (1994). *The Red Queen*. London: Penguin.

RITVO, L. (1990). *L'ascendant de Darwin sur Freud*. Paris: Gallimard.

ROSOLATO, G. (1967). Étude des perversions sexuelles à partir du fétichisme. *Le désir et la perversion*. Paris: Seuil, pp. 7-52.

SACHER-MASOCH, L. von (1996). *Venus in Furs*. London: Senate.

SCHOTTE, J. (1990). *Szondi avec Freud. Sur la voie d'une psychiatrie pulsionnelle.* Bibliothéque de patho-analyse. Brussels: Editions Universitaires De Boeck.
SCHREBER, D.P. (2000). *Memoirs of my Nervous Illness.* New York: New York Review Books.
SOLMS, M. (2002). *The Brain and the Inner World.* New York: Other Press.
SOLMS, M. & SALING, M. (1986). On psychoanalysis and neuroscience: Freud's attitude to the localizationist tradition. *Int. J. Psycho-Anal.* 67: 397-416.
SOPHOCLES (1994). *Antigone. The Women of Trachis. Philoctetes. Oedipus at Colonus.* London: Harvard University Press.
STOLLER, R. (1975). *Perversion.* New York: Pantheon Books
—. (1984). *Sex and gender.* London: Karnac Books
—. (1985). *Observing the Erotic Imagination.* New Haven: Yale University Press.
SULLOWAY, F. (1979). *Freud, Biologist of the Mind.* New York: Basic Books.
SZONDI, L. (1952). *Triebpathologie vol.1: Elemente der exakten Triebpsychologie und Triebpsychiatrie.* Bern: Hans Huber Verlag
—. (1963). *Schicksalsanalytische Therapie.* Bern: Hans Huber Verlag
VANDERMEERSCH, P. (1991). *Unresolved Questions in the Freud/Jung Debate: On Psychosis, Sexual Identity and Religion.* Leuven: Leuven University Press.
VAN HAUTE, Ph. (2002). *Against adaptation: Lacan's subversion of the subject.* New York: Other Press
—. & GEYSKENS, T. (2002). *Spraakverwarring. Het primaat van de seksualiteit bij Freud, Ferenczi en Laplanche.* Nijmegen: SUN. (English translation: (2004) *Confusion of tongues. The primacy of sexuality in Freud, Ferenczi and Laplanche.* New York: Other Press)
WINNICOTT, D.W. (1971). *Playing and Reality.* London: Tavistock/Routledge.
—. (1989). *Psycho-Analytic Explorations.* Harvard: Harvard Univ. Press.

www.ingramcontent.com/pod-product-compliance
Ingram Content Group UK Ltd.
Pitfield, Milton Keynes, MK11 3LW, UK
UKHW021834140426
5217IPUK00021B/1444